The Witches' Almanac

Spring 2018—Spring 2019

CONTAINING pictorial and explicit delineations of the
magical phases of the Moon together with information about astrological
portents of the year to come and various aspects of occult knowledge
enabling all who read to improve their lives in the old manner.

The Witches' Almanac, Ltd.

Publishers   Providence, Rhode Island
www.TheWitchesAlmanac.com

Address all inquiries and information to
THE WITCHES' ALMANAC, LTD.
P.O. Box 1292
Newport, RI   02840-9998

10-ISBN: 1-881098-43-5

13-ISBN: 978-1-881098-43-0

E-Book 13-ISBN: 978-1-881098-44-7

ISSN: 1522-3184

First Printing July 2017

Printed in USA

Established 1971 by Elizabeth Pepper

Preface

ELIZABETH PEPPER ONCE SAID, "My dear, do not shy from bad weather, but walk tall in the rain and embrace its gift."

It is now time to put aside the negativity that has been swirling around the world and embrace the gift of change. Move with change; do not resist. The Great Mother stirs and we will joyfully move with Her.

Gwydion Pendderwen recorded *The Lord of the Dance*, with variant lyrics, on his album *Songs of the Old Religion* (though, not the entire song). The lyrics can be found in various places, nonetheless here is an excerpt for you to sing or hum happily throughout the year, and knowing the Earth is changing and we are part of that change*. Celebrate!

> When she danced on the waters and the wind was her horn,
> The Lady laughed and everything was born,
> She lit the Sun and the Light gave him birth,
> The Lord of the Dance then appeared on the Earth,
>
> *Chorus*
> Dance then wherever you may be,
> For I am the Lord of the Dance, said He,
> And I'll lead you all wherever you may be,
> And I'll lead you on in the Dance, said He.
>
> I danced in the morning when the world was begun,
> I danced in the moon and the stars and the sun,
> I was called from the darkness by the song of the Earth,
> I joined in the singing and she gave me birth,

*Visit TheWitchesAlmanac.com/almanac-extras/ to hear a rendition of *The Lord of the Dance*

❧ HOLIDAYS ❧

Spring 2018 to Spring 2019

March 20 . . . . Vernal Equinox
April 1 . . . . All Fools' Day
April 30 . . . . Walpurgis Night
May 1 . . . . Beltane
May 8 . . . . White Lotus Day
May 9, 11, 13 . . . . Lemuria
May 29 . . . . Vesak Day
May 29 . . . . Oak Apple Day
June 5 . . . . Night of the Watchers
June 21 . . . . Summer Solstice
June 24 . . . . Midsummer
July 23 . . . . Ancient Egyptian New Year
July 31 . . . . Lughnassad Eve
August 1 . . . . Lammas
August 13 . . . . Diana's Day
August 16 . . . . Black Cat Appreciation Day
September 13 . . . . Ganesh Festival
September 22 . . . . Autumnal Equinox
October 31 . . . . Samhain Eve
November 1 . . . . Hallowmas
November 16 . . . . Hecate Night
December 16 . . . . Fairy Queen Eve
December 17 . . . . Saturnalia
December 21 . . . . Winter Solstice
January 9 . . . . Feast of Janus
February 1 . . . . Oimelc Eve
February 2 . . . . Candlemas
February 15 . . . . Lupercalia
March 1 . . . . Matronalia
March 19 . . . . Minerva's Day

Art Director . . . . Gwion Vran

Astrologer . . . . Dikki-Jo Mullen

Climatologist . . . . Tom C. Lang

Cover Art and Design . . . . Kathryn Sky-Peck

Marketing Manager . . . . N. Bullock

Sales . . . . Ellen Lynch

Shipping, Bookkeeping . . . . . D. Lamoureux

ANDREW THEITIC
Executive Editor

GREG ESPOSITO
Managing Editor

JEAN MARIE WALSH
Associate Editor

ANTHONY TETH
Copy Editor

CONTENTS

☙ CONTENTS ❧

And for witches,
This is law —
Where they enter in,
From *there* must they
withdraw.

Yesterday, Today and Tomorrow

by Timi Chasen

BREATHING TIME An Assistant Professor from Harvard Medical School has been showing the world how regular meditation and mindfulness practices have profoundly positive effects upon brain function and structure.

In a documentary called *The Connection*, as well as in an interview with the *Washington Post*, Mass General Hospital neuroscientist Sarah Lazar explains how MRI imaging has been able to demonstrably show the benefits of meditation, and how routine practice can change both brain chemistry and quality of life.

Studying two separate groups of individuals over a span of merely eight weeks, with one engaged in a regimen of regular meditation and the other not, Lazar was able to find increased brain activity and the thickening of tissue in areas of the brain associated with learning, memory, empathy, visualization, cognition and compassion, while noting a marked lessening of activity in those areas of the brain that monitor stress and anxiety.

This victory means more mindfulness studies are sure to come, as Harvard and other Ivy-League institutions such as Brown University are tasking some of their best and brightest in the Religion, Psychology, and Neuroscience departments to dig even deeper.

However, we at *The Witches' Almanac* see it as another instance of modern science "verifying" something that mystics have been saying for thousands of years.

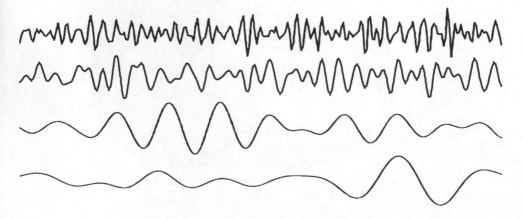

THE MEDIEVAL PYRAMIDS OF EAST ST. LOUIS

While Europe was dealing with the tumultuous invasions of the Dark Ages, cyclopean mounds and towering pyramids were being constructed alongside the swamplands of the Mississippi River. Immigration to this new settlement began in earnest around 900 CE, as thousands flocked from miles around.

The city was thriving by 1100 and would have had a population of approximately thirty thousand people—larger than both Paris and London at the time. Officially, it is currently deemed the largest pre-Columbian city found within continental US territory.

Located in Southern Illinois, the ancient settlement would have hugged the river, stretching approximately six square miles in size and encompassing a large chunk of land between modern Collinsville and East St. Louis.

The city's name, Cahokia, was given by European explorers who encountered a tribe of Native Americans in the 1600s who controlled the region. However, the Cahokia tribe claimed no affiliation with the city, which had been abandoned centuries prior. The name of the people who actually constructed it is still, unfortunately, lost.

The remains of the once-great city are now considered a National Historic Landmark. The 2,200 acre Cahokia Mounds National Historic Site remains open to visitors, and has been deemed a UNESCO World Heritage Site.

DOWNTOWN SERPENT TEMPLE

Further south in the heart of Mexico City, another ancient monument is being revealed layer by layer. Discovered not far from downtown's

Zocalo Plaza on the grounds of a 1950s hotel, the temple complex has archaeologists, historians and mystics wringing their hands in excitement.

Built during the reign of emperor Ahuizotl near the end of the 15th century, this huge and circular sacred structure was dedicated to Ehecatl, the Aztec deity of the winds, and included a ball court where religious games were played in his honor. The design of the court appears in alignment with much of the original Spanish chronicle of the region, which described some of the contests in question. Also found was a pile of thirty-two sets of human neck vertebrae—sacrifices in relation to the games.

Archaeologists claim the full complex was most probably designed to look like a massive coiled snake, with temple priests using a door situated in its nose.

BENNU AND OSIRIS The United States government sending a probe to intercept and study a possibly dangerous asteroid before returning home with its findings sounds a lot like the plot to a science fiction film. Make the names of both the 500-meter celestial stone and the state-of-the-art, unmanned space vessel inspired by Egyptian mythology, and one might think we've uncovered a lost episode of *Stargate*. However, in 2016 this is precisely what happened.

The carbonaceous sphere originally classified as 1999 RQ36 was given its Kemetic moniker after a "Name That Asteroid" contest. Bennu was a mystical, heron-like bird deity which featured heavily in the differing myth structures of the Ancient Egyptians. The latest readings seem to suggest there's a slim chance—about 0.04% by some estimates—that Bennu the rocky orb could collide with Earth in a couple

of centuries. Thus, NASA has sent its latest technological marvel to learn as much as it can—OSIRIS-REx. The research vessel will reach Bennu early on in 2018 and then spend the next 505 days mapping and collecting samples from the heavenly object, as well as leaving a time capsule with art, music and poetry, in case someone else happens along while it's away.

The OSIRIS-REx probe is due to return to Terra in 2023, when a team of awaiting international scientists shall analyze its fascinating finds.

BETTER LATE THAN NEVER
Canada has finally updated its criminal code, allowing Witches to practice their craft without theoretically being guilty of violating Section 365, which prohibited the use of "any kind of witchcraft, sorcery, enchantment or conjuration." A distant remnant of Old World religious paranoia, the antiquated statute also specifically made fortune-telling and the divination of lost and/or stolen items punishable by law.

Conveniently, over the past few decades, the law has been mostly forgotten except in a few cases of blatant fraud, where Canadian citizens had been the prey of pseudo-psychic scam artists. In these cases, Section 365 was used to add more legal weight to the sentencing in question.

However, the Canadian Pagan communities have been outspoken in their disdain for the law, since it obviously not only infringes upon religious freedom but criminalizes things as innocuous as Tarot readings. Thankfully, the government has heard their grievances and are overhauling it, along with other centuries-old laws no longer relevant to today's age, such as stipulations concerning dueling.

News from The Witches' Almanac

Glad tidings from the staff

At long last we have implemented our a new shopping cart. Drop by TheWitchesAlmanac.com, there is plenty to look at, in addition to some fun bells and whistles. We have consolidated many informational features into the new *Resources*. In addition to *Seasonal Recipes, Sites of Awe* and *Almanac Extras*, you will find *Author Bios*, *In Memoriam* and *Merry Meetings*. These new features are tributes to those who have impacted our community, as well as contributing to *The Witches Almanac*. The new site will allow us to promote special reductions, bundle discounts and more (allowing us to occasionally offer free shipping on select titles). But most of all, the new flexibility allows us to respond to the needs of our readership.

In January we brought you a wonderful new tome, Paul Huson's *Dame Fortune's Wheel Tarot*. Based upon Huson's research in *Mystical Origins of the Tarot*, *Dame Fortune's Wheel Tarot* illustrates for the first time the earliest, traditional Tarot card interpretations unadorned by the occult speculations of Mathers, Waite or Crowley. Rather Huson provides intepretations as collected in the 1700s by Jean-Baptiste Alliette, a Parisian fortune-teller otherwise known as Etteilla. In addition to detailed descriptions of the cards' symbolism and significance—with both regular and reversed meanings—Dame Fortune's Wheel Tarot provides meticulous full color reproductions of Huson's original designs for all 79 cards, including an extra Significator card as specified by Etteilla that may be used optionally. Dame Fortune's Wheel Tarot also provides full instructions for laying out the cards for divination.

Many of you may not be aware that we maintain a brick & mortar presence at the Troll Shop in East Greenwich, Rhode Island. We have expanded our section in this fine store. Stop by if you are in the neighborhood. Not only do we offer most of titles, you can browse the wonderful selection of handmade trolls offered by the shop.

The coming year promises to be a big year for us. We have several titles queued up for publication. Before the end of 2017 into early 2018, *The Witches' Almanac* is planning to bring two classics to press, as well as a scholarly publication on folk magic and perhaps a new title from a beloved elder of Witchcraft.

As always, we are happy to be working with you, our readership. In an effort to improve your experience with *The Witches' Almanac*, we will continue to grow and evolve as the magical community does.

www.TheWitchesAlmanac.com

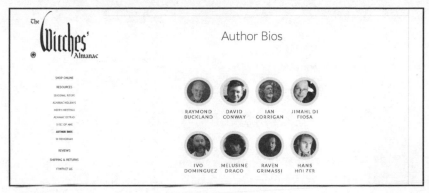

Come visit us at the **new** Witches' Almanac website

POMBA GIRA

Queen of the Kalunga

DEEP WITHIN THE *favelas* (poor neighborhoods) of Brazil or a second story apartment in the Bronx of New York City between the hours of midnight and dawn can be heard the *pontos cantados* (ritual songs) accompanied by the scents of cigars, cigarettes and cachaça (raw rum). Those within dance in a whirling motion while smoking and swigging hard liquor, inviting to join them the male Exu spirits and female Pomba Gira spirits of the Brazilian sorcery cult known as Quimbanda (or Kimbanda.)

An ever-evolving system with three main roots—European, African and South American, Quimbanda is Brazil's gift to the realm of New World sorcery. From Europe come the Grimoire traditions and classic Christian imagery of the Devil and Infernal spirits. Its African roots come mainly from the sorcery-laden Congo traditions, which serve as the foundation of ritual and the various vessels in which the spirits dwell. Many South American Native spirits have also found a home within this spiritual current and make up at least one entire line or family of spirits. The syncretic nature of Quimbanda is a source of its power as it is always reinventing itself, never staying still, coiling and uncoiling like a pit of vipers.

The history and modern manifestation of Quimbanda is beautifully complex and the different *cabulas* (houses or congregations) vary greatly in form and practice. Sometimes dark adjuncts to Candomble or Umbanda houses and sometimes stand-alone structures of nocturnal dealings, one thing they all have in common is the multitude of Exus and Pomba Giras petitioned for love, money, protection and the entire spectrum of human existence. There are hundreds if not thousands of these spirits honored and called upon, and each one has his or her distinct personality and menu of offerings.

While the Exus draw from the recognizably devilish and demonic masculine aesthetic, the Pomba Giras appear in a wide array of lesser-known or overshadowed female roles like the royal mistress, the sorceress, the gypsy, the prostitute, the bar owner and the warrior, to name but a few. The figures polite society disapproves of and tries to prevent its daughters from becoming, the Pomba Giras come from the spirits of princesses who where never rescued and who had to rescue themselves, becoming strong, respected and feared in the process. They are just as powerful as their male counterparts and generally speaking it is said that Pomba Gira has seven husbands, all of whom she dominates.

Pomba Gira Maria Padilha, the Queen of the Castle; Pomba Gira Maria Mulambo, the Patron of the Poor and Widows; Pomba Gira Rainha das Sete Encruzilhadas, Queen of the Seven Crossroads; Pomba Gira Cigana, the Gypsy; Pomba Gira Rainha do Inferno, the Queen of Hell; Pomba Gira Rosa Caveira, the half skull-faced Witch and Warrior. These are but a fraction of the feminine forces found within the amazingly complex Lines, Kingdoms and Roads of Quimbanda. Pomba Gira truly is Legion.

Confident in her sexuality and deadly with her sensuality, Pomba Gira does not shy away from the delights of the flesh. In some forms she proudly displays her exposed breasts and dares anyone to suggest she show modesty by covering them. In most forms her sharp tongue can shred the most macho of men to ribbons in a matter of seconds as she turns to seduce the next one without even adjusting her crown. The force of her personality never wavers and she never second guesses herself. She is that person many aspire to be, but fear or societal pressures keep us from becoming.

Each of us has a ruling Pomba Gira (and Exu) and the best way to discover her is to receive a consultation from a Tata Quimbanda (male priest) or Yaya Quimbanda (female priestess). Most times the consultation will reveal many more of the Infernal spirits that walk beside us in the shadows, including a

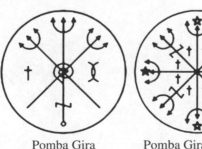 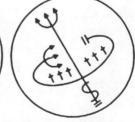

Pomba Gira   Pomba Gira Menina   Pomba Gira Cigana

"working" Exu and Pomba Gira, and as is their nature the reasons why we have them may not always be clear. What is clear, though, is that they can be either powerful forces of change or the skeleton keys of our personal self-destruction. The choice is ours.

Lacking a formal consultation, a person can, if so inclined, honor one or more of the Pomba Giras in very simple ways. For example, if you feel drawn to a particular Pomba Gira, find her ponto riscado or seal and gather together a square piece of red fabric, usually no larger than a foot squared, a piece of white chalk, a small red taper candle, a red rose, a shot glass, some cachaça or white rum and a Virginia Slim or clove cigarette. If you can do this at night and in that Pomba Gira's kingdom, such as a crossroad, cemetery, beach, etc., all the better. If you can't, you can do this somewhere in your home to leave overnight and then gather up to take to that kingdom the next day. Lay the red cloth on the ground and draw her ponto riscado on it with the chalk. Place the red candle, rose and shot glass with libation on the ponto riscado. Light the candle and the cigarette and place the cigarette across the top of the shot glass. Call to her simply and from the heart. Ask her to accept the offerings and give you a sign that she has done so. You can remain a while to see if you feel a presence around you—you may or may not. The sign may come later in the form of a dream. When you are done say a word of thanks and ask that no malevolent spirits follow you or remain in your home if you do this indoors. If outdoors, leave the area without looking back.

I strongly recommend finding a Tata or Yaya to guide you should you wish to go further with Quimbanda. I also offer a word of warning before delving into the darkness of the Kalunga, the oceanic realm of the dead that permeates the physical realm—home to many denizens of the Infernal Fig Tree. The Pomba Giras don't play unless it's for their own amusement, many times to our detriment. Their presence is impressive and without filter, revealing many things about ourselves we wish to keep hidden or deny.

Stripping us down to our bare bones, exposing the lies we've told ourselves, Pomba Gira takes a drag off her cigarette and laughs. This is for the purpose of making us grow stronger than we thought possible, a tough love in sometimes the most cruel of ways. My Tata says "Quimbanda itself will always betray those it holds dear that they may grow. It is a cult of vicious honesty. If we are anything less than honest with ourselves, they will rake and tear at us until only truth remains."

—STEVEN W. BRAGG

THIS DAY, O SOUL

Tenderly—be not impatient,

(Strong is your hold, O mortal flesh,

Strong is your hold O love.)

THIS day, O Soul, I give you a wondrous mirror;

Long in the dark, in tarnish and cloud it lay—But the cloud has

pass'd, and the tarnish gone;

... Behold, O Soul! it is now a clean and bright mirror,

Faithfully showing you all the things of the world.

WALT WHITMAN

THE THIRTEEN MOST HAUNTED CITIES IN THE USA

The Witches' Almanac's Top Picks for Ghost Hunters

"You should come back tonight and do the ghost tour. There are lots of ghosts around here always."

"Oh, how cool."

THIS CONVERSATION snippet was overheard while waiting in line to tour the historic and reputedly haunted St. Augustine Lighthouse and Maritime Museum in Florida. The speakers were a ticket sales agent and teenage customer who had asked whether the lighthouse was really haunted as his wrist band was being attached. The yellow wrist bands, which allow admission to one of the famous historic sites in St. Augustine, read "Dark of the Moon Ghost Tours, More than Just Stories." The special evening event at that lighthouse is just one of the hundreds of ghost tours offered in nearly every city across the United States. Most places are at least a bit haunted. Lingering spirits attached to the scenes of events both tragic and joyful are subjects of universal intrigue. *The Witches' Almanac* has painstakingly

considered cities throughout the country to determine which are the thirteen most haunted—the best picks for ghost hunters. This was quite a challenge as paranormal investigation to evaluate spirit activity is ephemeral, contingent upon timing and individual sensitivity. Ghost enthusiasts might not completely agree with these choices, but each of them offers excellent ghost tours with documentation of messages and visitations from the afterlife. Thirteen finalists have been selected as a nod to the mystery and magic associated with the number thirteen and its longtime link to witchery. Key Thirteen in the Tarot deck is the Death card.

13. Eureka Springs, Arkansas

This Victorian spa village in the Ozark mountains is home to The Crescent Hotel, which claims to be the most haunted hotel in the country. The hotel was built in 1886 as a hospital where con artist Dr. Douglas Baker claimed to have found a cure for cancer. So many patients died that bodies were smuggled out late at night for dis-

posal. The former morgue is a stop on the ghost tour where many apparitions have been sighted. A child with pigtails in a yellow dress, a nurse and a figure surrounded by mist are a few. The hot mineral-laden springs have attracted those seeking healing and enhanced spirituality for centuries, so many linger.

12. Deadwood, South Dakota
This legendary Old West town takes its name from a gulch of dead trees which lined the area where gold was discovered. Wild Bill Hickok, Calamity Jane and other characters linked to its gun fights, saloons, gambling and dance halls lived in, died in and have remained to haunt Deadwood. Native American wars also figure prominently in the haunted history of the area.

11. Virginia Beach, Virginia
Strategically located along the shores of Chesapeake Bay, Virginia Beach was settled by Captain John Smith in 1607 and has been associated with various significant events. The Golden Age of Piracy, centering around the exploits of Blackbeard, numerous shipwrecks as well as battles generate reports of paranormal activity. Grace Sherwood, the Witch of Pungo, was tried and convicted of Witchcraft in Virginia Beach on July 10, 1706. The sky was a clear blue when Grace was tossed into the water, dunked with her thumbs tied to her toes. Immediately dark clouds gathered and a fearsome storm began. The Witch miraculously freed herself and swam to shore, angrily cursing her captors. She lived another half century or so and has ever since been one of the ghosts associated with this coastal town.

10. Seattle, Washington
For thousands of years Seattle was sacred to the Suquamish and Duwamish indigenous tribes. This city is built on ancient burial grounds, marking the beginning of its long, rich history with a dark side. It was later bloodied by the Grand Army of the Republic. Cries and shouts of soldiers, Native Americans and fortune hunters have been recorded. Apparitions are plentiful near the Pike Place Market and the West Seattle High School. A heartbroken student named Rose Higginbotham hanged herself at the school in 1924 and is reputed to wander the halls still.

9. Lewes, Delaware
Called "The First City in the First State," Lewes is historically linked to the War of 1812 and a series of maritime tragedies. The Cannon Ball House, now a museum, was built in 1765 and is still in its original location. A cannon ball, believed to have been fired by the British in April, 1813, remains lodged in the wall of this haunted

house. At least 800 souls have been lost at sea during the past few centuries off the coast near Lewes. Numerous apparitions and ghostly encounters have been recorded near the ferry terminal where boats commuting from Cape May, New Jersey arrive daily.

8. Santa Fe, New Mexico

A multiplicity of cultures shaped this Western city which was founded in 1610 and claims to be the oldest State Capital in the USA. Its name translates to "Holy Faith"—a renaming of an ancient Native American settlement at the location called "White Shell Water Place." As many as 20 different ghosts during a three-hour period have been recorded by paranormal investigators studying phenomena in this picturesque Colonial city. Located on the Santa Fe Trail, a busy route for travelers during the opening up of the West, tales of a zombie outbreak in the 1880s, visits from outlaws including Billy the Kid and even a visit from St. Joseph figure in the haunt history of Santa Fe. In 1878 a beautiful chapel built in France was transported to Santa Fe and assembled. There was a problem, however—there was no way for the nuns to access the choir loft, 22 feet above the floor. Local builders shook their heads, saying the only way up would be to climb a ladder. Legend tells that the sisters

began to pray and a stranger, a craftsman, arrived. He constructed a mysterious spiral staircase that seems to be balanced on air, built from an extinct type of wood and held together by only wooden pegs. When the master carpenter disappeared without collecting his pay, it was speculated that he was actually St. Joseph. Over the years, architects and engineers have been unable to ever explain the construction of the ghostly stairway which still stands in the Chapel of Loretto. It was featured on the television show "Unsolved Mysteries."

7. Savannah, Georgia

Founded in 1733 as a debtors' prison by the British, Savannah is the oldest city in Georgia. Its coastal location made it a strategic location for military activity during the Revolutionary War. Atop the ruins of graves and debris twenty-two park-like squares were built, surrounded by beautiful buildings and connected by cobblestone streets. Savannah offers multiple unique and authentic ghost tours, including a delightful haunted pub crawl. Tour guides claim the entire city is a graveyard as they recount a variety of creepy events. The Sorrel-Weed House, circa 1837, is a major paranormal activity hub where visitors can experience overnight ghost investigations.

6. Salem, Massachusetts

Dubbed "The Witch City" for its connection to the infamous trials, Salem has an extensive documented history of spectral happenings and ghostly sightings. One of the many available tours introduces thirteen different ghosts. Hot spots include The House of the Seven Gables; the subject of Nathaniel Hawthorne's novel *Gallows Hill*, where the condemned were hanged and the Witch House. This was the home and court room of the infamous Judge Corwin who presided over the trials. It is the only structure still standing which is linked to the 17th Century witch scare. Now a museum, the Witch House depicts life as it was when the Judge held court there.

5. St. Augustine, Florida

The oldest city in the continental United States, St. Augustine was founded in 1565. The city prides itself on its sheer volume of historic sites dating back to the discovery of the Fountain of Youth by Ponce De Leon in 1513 and for the non-theatrical, authentic ghost tours it offers. Ghostly voices, orbs captured in photos and spectral visitors on film are abundant. The Castillo de San Marcos, a massive fort built by the Spanish about 1672, has a tiny room where the spirit of a wayward wife walled up alive by an angry husband can be encountered. At the Old City Gate a ghost named Elizabeth who

perished from yellow fever appears. She signals to visitors whether it is safe or not to enter. The Lighthouse provides a refuge for the many spirits of light keepers and their families who call it home still. The Gonzalez-Alvarez House, built in the 1700s, is the oldest surviving Spanish Colonial home. Several of its original tenants have remained. The Spanish Military Hospital is another very active site which is well worth visiting.

4. Chicago, Illinois

Chicago's dynamic energy field was summed up by Mark Twain in 1883 when he wrote: "It is hopeless for the occasional visitor to keep up with Chicago, she outgrows his prophecies faster than he can make them." The city's name is adopted from *Shikaakwa* its Potawatomi Indian name, meaning "wild onion or garlic." The haunt history probably began when the Native American inhabitants were killed or forcibly removed by European settlers in the early 1830s. The famous large fire supposedly started by Catherine O'Leary's cow, gangster hangouts, mob

of life. Examples include a yellow fever epidemic in 1853 which left almost eight thousand dead, their bodies stacked in the streets. More recently there was Hurricane Katrina. Sailors arriving ashore with cash to spend were often crime victims. The slave market, a place of incredible cruelty and hangings, ushered in the Voudoun tradition. The consumption of alcohol created emotional dramas, leading to tragedies. Elaborate jazz funerals and historic cemeteries call the attention of ghosts. Then there is the warm, steamy climate. This creates a relaxed daydream-like state of mind and enhanced alpha brain waves, allowing investigators to attune to the spirit world. Arnaud's, a famous restaurant in the historic French Quarter, is said to be haunted by the ghost of Germaine, the original owner's daughter. Germaine, who managed the restaurant after Count Arnaud's death, has remained after her own death to admire her collection of Mardi Gras memorabilia. The Bourbon Orleans Hotel, another top stop for paranormal investigators, seems to be very haunted by the ghosts of children. It was once an orphanage. Then of course there is the "Voodoo Queen" Marie Laveau and numerous other spirit visitors.

shootings and a variety of other wild, frightening situations followed to contribute to Chicago's haunted reputation. Highly regarded paranormal investigators have authenticated Chicago's hauntings, including the ghosts active at Oprah Winfrey's studio. Resurrection Mary is a hitchhiking ghost whom many have encountered over the years.

3. New Orleans, Louisiana

A paranormal gumbo of ghostly activity offers a genuine welcome wagon to the droves of ghost hunters who visit New Orleans. Located where the Mississippi River flows into the Gulf of Mexico, the city is surrounded by murky swamps and water, offering an energy conduit. Every half century or so since its founding in the 17th Century, a major tragedy has led to massive destruction of property and loss

2. New York City, New York

"There is more of everything here than there is anywhere else," a native New Yorker once said.

The above often seems to hold true when it comes to meeting the ghosts of the Big Apple. Every single street in New York is steeped in four centuries of colorful history. Almost from the very beginning, long before ghost hunting became chic, encounters with the spirit world were frequently reported throughout New York City, from Washington Heights to Staten Island. The Brooklyn Bridge is connected to many paranormal episodes. Edgar Allen Poe spent much of his life in Greenwich Village, where he wrote "The Raven." One of the places where his apparition appears is Poe Cottage—once his home, now a museum.

1. Washington, DC

Often called the most haunted capital city in the entire world, Washington, DC is a regular hub of paranormal activity. It is our number one pick. From Capitol Hill, with underground vaults guarding untold secrets, to the White House, where Abraham Lincoln's ghost startles guests by knocking on the door of his old office (now a bedroom), to Arlington Cemetery, the National Mall and Georgetown, spirit activity is abundant. The ghost of Dolley Madison appears at several different locations. The title "First Lady" was coined for Dolley and she has been seen in the White House Rose Garden which she originally planted. Dolley also likes to return to visit the Octagon House, where she and her husband President James Madison lived after the British burned the White House in 1812. Ghost tours in the District of Columbia are carefully authenticated and highlighted with enjoyable historic anecdotes.

—SUE LEROY

Thumb Cats

Polydactyls

CATS ARE EXOTIC creatures. They move like silk, purr like thunder and sit motionless as they regard us with an inscrutable gaze. They can be aloof mannequins, sitting still enough for us to mistake them for a statue, or running around like crazy hellions, bouncing off the furniture and drapes.

Earlier societies who viewed these strange traits and the cats' nocturnal habits as signs of devilment must have found it terrifying to see that some even appeared to be growing thumbs.

Mitten Kittens
Commonly called thumb cats, mitten cats, six-fingered cats or snowshoe cats, these unusual felines are more properly called polydactyl cats, from the Greek *poly*, meaning many and *daktulos*, meaning fingered. Some incorrectly refer to these as "double-pawed" cats, which is a different paw condition. With true double-pawed cats, two mirror image paws are fused together.

Whereas normal cats possess five toes on each front paw and four toes on each rear paw, polydactyl cats can have as many as eight or ten toes on a paw. In 2002 a veterinarian counted a total of 28 toes on a cat from Canada named Jake, enough to make him a Guinness World Record holder. His extra appendages were distributed evenly among his four paws— seven on each.

When the extra digit appears on the side of the paw, like an opposable thumb, it helps a cat with its grasp.

Felines and Brine
Because their extra toes help them hold steady on a rolling ship, sailors

favored multi-toed cats for ship's cats. Though they can't quite climb the rigging like a movie-style pirate, they can grasp a rope, just as they can grasp prey. On a ship, good mousers were well-prized. Mice and rats proliferate rapidly and head for the grain storage. Besides eating the grain, they urinate and defecate on it, making the grain no longer fit for human consumption. When you're weeks out at sea and have no form of radio communication, you can't just call out for pizza when you run out of edible food.

Their usefulness as mousers might be the reason cats were considered good luck for sailors. The multi-toed cats on board reproduced, their offspring being blessed with the same harmless genetic mutation causing extra toes.

Upon arriving at their destination, male cats found it easy to disembark while the ship was unloading. Eager to investigate new worlds, they also discovered mates among the local cat population, leaving their genetic mark on the resulting litters of kittens. The fact that this mutation is often found near seaports along the East Coast of North America (in the United States and Canada) tends to support this theory. Though some sources state these cats are rare in Europe because they were killed as witches' familiars, they are quite common along the coast in South West England and Wales, and inland ports like Kingston-upon-Hull. Multi-toed cats were so popular in the former Welsh county of Cardiganshire (now Ceredigion) that the cats are often called Cardi-cats.

Colonial Kitties

Some believe polydactyl cats came to the United States on the Mayflower or even earlier, with 11th-century Norse sailors who visited the Maine coast seeking timber and trade, especially since the Maine Coon cat, a native breed prone to polydactyly, strongly resembles the Norwegian Forest cat.

Polydactyly was a useful evolutionary adaptation for Maine cats. Double toes act as natural snowshoes, useful in harsh Maine winters. At one time this peculiarity occurred in as much as 40% of the Maine Coon population. The occurrence of the trait fell over the years as cat clubs and other breeding associations listed the trait as unfavorable. Lately though, some clubs have started to allow it again.

In New Zealand a new polydactyl cat breed called the Clippercat is being recognized and developed under strict guidelines. The greatest concentration of this genetic mutation is found near Auckland and in the Hauraki Gulf where, between 1850 and 1900, Clipper Ships made the rounds between England and the Antipodes.

Regardless of their origin or what you call them, there's something magickal when one of these creatures gently wraps all those toes around your finger in a loving caress.

—MORVEN WESTFIELD

ucke. Men
thus call a
merrie litel
Elfe or Faery
and Puckrels
be verie smal
Pucks which
appeare in
Glasses or Cristalls or Rings. But old
Dame Darrel would have none
of this. for she said that of later
times Elues and Sprights and
Gobblins which were of yore all
different are now all called
one by the others' name as som
wene that all Buggs be nightmares

Excerpt from

The Witchcraft of Dame Darrel of York

Pucke. Men thus call a merrie litel Elve or Faery, and Puckrels be verie smal Pucks which appeare in Glasses or Cristalls or Rings. But old *Dame Darrel would have none of this. for she said that of later times Elves and Sprights and Gobblins which were of* yore all different, are now all called one by the others' Name as som wene that all Buggs be Nighmares

OFFICE MAGIC

USING CONSERVATIVE mathematics, an individual working a full-time job outside the home spends an average of 2,080 hours a year in a workplace environment. In most cases, the aesthetics of this environment are controlled by others. While many employers are trying nowadays to create more user friendly, ergonomically designed workplaces, many more are still set up based on an old school institutional standard of focusing not on employee comfort but on maximum employee productivity.

Perhaps for a magical person, the challenges of functioning well inside a work environment are felt more acutely. At home we can control most every aspect of our living space. We can surround ourselves with sacred objects, favorite photographs and inspirational artwork. Fresh flowers on the dining table and lighting a stick of incense work wonders in assisting us to maintain balance and harmony.

The work place, however, may present more of a challenge. It is not usually a place we can control, but a foreign country whose borders and interiors are influenced by other entities. Its purpose is not to make us feel warm and fuzzy but to keep us focused on the meeting or exceeding the goals of the employer.

However, building a discreet, magical comfort zone within a business environment is much easier than most people realize. Here are some helpful hints.

Remember your happy space
We all have a "happy space"—a place in our mind that helps us to remember the simple joys of life. A beach, a secluded clearing in the forest, a mountain top or a secret location in a busy city. Whether you work in a cubicle or a physical office space, it is important to remember your happy space and to go there often. Try to find an image, no matter how small, that represents this special place in your mind. A post card, a small framed photograph or an object such as a shell or stone can be used to trigger your imagination and help you

to retreat to this private space whenever you need to mentally recharge. It can be a real stress reliever when needed.

Calendars

Using the same thought process as above, try to pick out an annual calendar that focuses on a favorite theme. For example, if your secret place is a garden, you may consider purchasing a calendar that features a new garden for every month. The image on the calendar will not only help you to remember that there is more to enjoy in life than your day job, but that time passes. Not even the toughest, grumpiest boss can stop the seasons from turning or prevent Friday from becoming the weekend.

Cafeteria Secrets

Many workplaces feature a café, cafeteria or break room. These areas provide many mundane objects that can be used to create magic in the workplace. A plastic knife can be used discreetly, with the proper intention, as a magical tool by which you can create sacred space. When feeling hassled by a co-worker or particularly stressed out by your boss, try discreetly creating a circle around your desk as you munch your sandwich. The plastic knife can also be placed inside desk drawers, point facing the entrance to your workspace, as a magical charm against harm.

Most magical practitioners recognize the value of salt in occult operations. Next time you're in the cafeteria, pick up a few extra packets of salt and keep them in your desk drawer. With very minimal intent, a packet of unopened salt will perform the same function as consecrated salt inside a magic circle—protect you from all ill intent while in possession of the packet.

Stress Management

We often encounter problems at work. Perhaps a co-worker, vying for attention from the higher ups, has said untruthful things about you, or maybe a particular situation at work has become very complicated.

You can regain control over any difficult situation by taking a standard paperclip and with magical intention, bending the paperclip back into a straight line. Focus as much energy on the tiny piece of metal as possible while holding an image of the desired outcome in your mind. If desired, place the straightened clip in your pocket, briefcase or desk drawer and touch it whenever you feel the need to reinforce your intent.

Binding Bands

Elastic bands can be used in extreme circumstances as a binding tool. When a situation seems to go from bad to worse, it is easy to neutralize negativity by making a discreet symbol that best characterizes the situation on a small piece of paper and then rolling the paper into a small scroll. Use the rubber band to "bind" the situation. It is best to make the band as tight as possible while focus-

ing your magical intent. Keep the object in your possession until the situation is resolved favorably, then discard.

Elemental Influences

Many magical people find some comfort in visualizing the elemental world around them. The powers of Earth, Air, Fire and Water are invaluable partners in magical endeavors. It is surprisingly easy to maintain images of the elemental world while in the workplace. A gemstone, such as quartz or amethyst, placed on your desk is very seldom viewed by others as a questionable object. Using it as a paper weight provides a perfect alibi to your true intention. Another trick is to focus on color correspondences as representations of the elements. Post-it notes, for example, come in a variety of colors, as do plastic thumb tacks. If a particular memo or policy needs to be posted prominently in an area you control, try placing a green, yellow, red and blue thumbtack at each of the four corners. At any point in time you will be able to look up at the poster and see instead "Earth, Air, Fire and Water."

Hopefully you will find both practical application and enjoyment in some of the techniques described above. Always remember that work, like other aspects of our lives, is what we choose to make it. Make your work place just more a bit more magical and the day will not only fly by but you'll leave with a smile on your face that will leave your co-workers very confused.

—JIMAHL DI FIOSA

Diabolous in Musica

A PIECE OF MUSIC by Niccolò Paganini features in an 1846 publication and is entitled *Air for the Flute: Incantation Dance of Witches under the Walnut Tree* of Benevento. The theme however is from Paganini's 1813 set of variations for solo violin and orchestra, *Le Streghe* which was itself inspired by the music of the ballet *Il noce di Benevento*, composed by Franz Xaver Sűssmayr.

The Walnut Tree of Benevento which inspired both these pieces is central to the story of the Duke of Benevento, who in 662 was persuaded by Saint Barbato to cut it down. The tree was believed to be the site of frequent Witch gatherings where a golden viper was venerated. The Witches, undeterred by the destruction of the tree, regrew it from seed and according to legend, it still stands to this day within the town. The viper was melted and turned into a chalice which was then used in the town's church.

Paganini (1782–1840) is one of the most well-known virtuoso violinists of his time and certainly one of the most controversial. It is therefore no surprise that a person who revelled in being called "Hexensohn" (Witch's child) would write music depicting Witch gatherings. The music Paganini composed and performed was of such complexity that many believed him to be in possession of abilities given by the Devil. The truth however was that Paganini suffered from Marfan syndrome which affected the connective tissue of his hands, enabling him to perform stretches and other extended violin techniques with ease.

Le Streghe was composed by Paganini in 1813 and takes its main

theme from Süssmayr (1766-1803) a composer and conductor perhaps best known for completing Mozart's *Requiem in D Minor*. The ballet focuses on the nocturnal gathering of Witches at the Walnut Tree in Benevento and was choreographed by Salvatore Viganò (1769–1821) who was the Ballet master of La Scala in 1804 and had previously studied composition with the renowned cellist Luigi Boccherini. The melody recreates the dancing of the Witches through its use of a 6/8 metre, uplifting tempo and leaping intervals.

Paganini was not the only composer to produce works influenced by tales and visions of Witchcraft. Tartini (1692–1770) wrote *The Devil's Trill Sonata* circa 1740 but it was not published until 1798—almost 30 years after his death. Upon its publication an annotation was included stating "The Devil at the foot of the bed" which references a dream Tartini had in 1713. Tartini's other manuscript annotations were written in a unique cipher which was not broken until 1935, but as the annotation was not some doubt is cast on its authenticity. It is believed that in this dream Tartini saw the Devil at the foot of his bed who then performed a piece for him on the violin. Upon waking, Tartini attempted to capture the piece he had heard and the result was the sonata. Tartini lamented his inability to adequately capture the beautiful piece he had experienced.

There is no question as to the virtuosity and compelling story of the *Devil's Trill Sonata*. Paganini would have surely been aware of it and in all likelihood, performed it. The sonata, Tartini, Paganini and their possible diabolical links are discussed in the second chapter of a short story by Madame Blavatsky called *The Ensouled Violin*. Wherever the influence for its composition may have derived from, the piece still has the ability to charm audiences as a concert encore today, almost 200 years after it was written and Paganini remains one of history's greatest violinists.

—JERA

32

Air for the Flute

Incantation Dance of Witches Under the Walnut Tree of Benevento

Nicolò Paganini

This tune may be heard on our website's Almanac Extras at: TheWitchesAlmanac.com/
diabolous.html./

Making Powders

MANY OF THE POWDERS sold to practitioners of magic are composed mainly of talc, which is problematic because it is a known carcinogen. Another common ingredient in commercial powders is called wood flour, finely ground up wood of unknown source—so it could be "pressure-treated" wood (i.e., poison). Why mess with these ingredients when you can make your own powders? Moreover, since an excellent main ingredient for homemade powders—and a traditional use of plant material in old-fashioned pharmacy—is stalks, they demonstrate a Witches' thrift. You can strip off the leaves of a dried plant and reserve those for teas, strewings, stuffings, vinegars, waters, or even incense. But you can keep the stalks to make powders.

Stalks are the bones of a plant; this analogy appears as far back as the Greek Magical Papyri. Once Witchcraft practice distinguishes between Living and Dead Bones when it comes to plants; I find these categories useful. Living Bones are green stalks, those that are living when they are harvested. When dried and ground, Living Bones make powders embodying the plant's more positive or friendly aspects.

Brown stalks—those that have gone through a winter or have turned brown because the plant experienced drought or disease—are considered Dead Bones. Dead Bones evoke the plant's more negative aspects (hostility, aggressiveness) or may simply be used in more negative magic. To make your life a little easier, cut the plant bones up before you dry them. Use secateurs for Living Bones and an

anvil pruner for Dead Bones. Even though Dead Bones are already dried, they may have dew or rain on them and should be put through the dehydrator to crisp them up. Plant material is easier to grind when it's crispy dry.

You can take this further by "mortifying" Dead Bones in several ways. You can perform what is basically a Black Toad operation using decay. This was the first stage in alchemical transformation, during which most of the impure aspects of a substance are destroyed by rotting or fermentation. To do this, wet them and seal them up (the smell of such an operation can be pretty atrocious). Think of the possibilities of various liquids used in the wetting—wine for deadly intoxication, urine for destruction, vinegar for sharpening or souring.

Another way to mortify a plant's qualities is to heat the bones until the plant material is blackened, turned to ash, or even calcined (when the white, caustic, alchemical salt of the plant is all that's left). To mortify with heat, put the Dead Bones in a little roasting pan in the oven at 450°F for half an hour or so. This can also be done outside on a fire. Some people use a torch lighter or even a propane torch. You can then add the resulting mortified bones to other items like incense or oils. They also make a good foundation for a magical powder.

You can tweak a powder by adding other bones, Living or Dead, and also by tossing the powder with essential oils and/or perfumes to modify or amplify the plant's energy. You can also add any items that don't work well in incense because they are noncombustible or smell bad when burned, like mint or orange peel. And you can play with noncombustible ingredients like iron oxide (brick dust, for Mars energy), glitter, mica, metallic powders, mineral powders, rocks, dirt or pigments. You can see how wide a range of possibilities you have beyond the basic dyed sawdust you so often find being sold in foil packets as condition powders in occult shops. Better tools help make better magic.

A powder needs an appropriate vessel, even more than an oil, a water, or an incense. The vibration, if you will, of a powder is more subtle and more easily disarranged. Since only a fairy-sized pinch is necessary for dressing candles, clothing, tools or other objects, a small vessel is usually adequate. A used antique jar makes a good container—just cense it first with the purifier of your choice. Mugwort is nice for this—it's everywhere; it's a Witch's staple herb; and it's a traditional friend of flame in herbalism.

—HAROLD ROTH
Excerpt from *The Witching Herbs*
(See review on page 189)

The Art of the Omen Days

Light from Midwinter's Heart

EVERY YEAR as Midwinter brings the holidays, we have the wonderful opportunity to enter the still-point of the fading year and emerge with fresh focus for the coming year. In some households the Omen Days are kept, which the rest of the world knows as 'the Twelve Days of Christmas.' Most people remember the carol about these days: 'On the first day of Christmas, my true love sent to me,' where a successive number of gifts arrive for each of the twelve days, with a multiplicity of birds, rings and people with their own special aptitudes.

These special days have a long history which stems from a time before they were adopted by the Christian world. In Brittany and Wales, the Twelve Days of Christmas which mark the intercalary days of the year are called the 'Omen Days,' and have a special purpose. 'Intercalary days' are really the days left over from reckoning up the solar year and in calendars throughout the world and at different times, they are special because they are considered to be 'the days out of time.' It is usually in this magical interval that Gods are born or conceived in many different mythologies, including the Irish divinity Oengus Og, who is conceived, grown and born at Brúg na Boinne (Newgrange in the Boyne Valley, Ireland) all in

one day by the skilful workings of the Dagda.

Within these twelve days lies a wonderful secret that anyone dismissive of the Christian tradition might well miss, for each of these twelve intercalary days is assigned to a month of the coming year, with the first day of Christmas on the 26th December as symbolic of January, the second day or 27th December representing February and so on, right through to 6th January which represents the December yet to come. It was the custom of many people in Brittany and Wales to go out on each of the Omen Days to observe the signs in nature and divine from them the state of the year to come. The omens experienced on each of the Omen Days indicated the nature of each month in the coming year.

We have to remember that whenever a newer tradition comes into a country, the older one doesn't just die or go away, but becomes fused with the newer so that a traditional, ancestral continuity of custom can be enjoyed by all. That the Omen Days have kept their assured place at the heart of Celtic divination is one of those wonderful instances of double-decker belief scattered throughout folk traditions worldwide, whereby aspects of an older belief continue beneath a new one. The Omen Days have been hiding under the Twelve Days of Christmas all this long while, waiting to be discovered. Tradition remembers that each of the Omen Days has a special gift attached to it. This wisdom can also be yours.

Reading The Omen Days

The divining of oracles from nature has a long tradition in Celtic lore. The Scots Gaelic tradition of the frith or augury from the signs of nature is well established. In this method, a seer would go to the door of the house, fasting and barefoot, with eyes closed. Making an invocation for clear sight, the seer would then open his or her eyes and see, framed within the lintels of the door which he or she grasped with either hand, some sign from nature. This might be a bird flying across the seer's field of vision or a fisherman coming from the boats, a sudden shower of rain, a woman gathering eggs from under the hens or a wild creature weaving through the bushes. By means of this frith the seer could foretell the nature of things for the community or household for the next quarter.

Few of the omens of ancient times have survived in written record since this was essentially an oracular art. So how might we do this today, when so many omens are lost? This practice can be done in any part of the world, using the omens and signs in nature. Even in cities nature shows itself to us, alongside other more urban signs which you should not ignore if they present themselves. The more your practice, the better you will be.

Anyone can do it, as long as they first ask a well-framed question or request. The question is the springboard of the answer—what you ask is what you get, as the whole universe, like an old camera, narrows the aperture for you to focus on what you need to see. The real skill is to read the signs in accordance with your understanding at the time and as it relates to the question that provoked the augury in the first place. You don't have to have an exact or particular knowledge of omens.

Treat each of the Omen Days as an augury opportunity for the month it represents in the coming year. Start on whatever day is good for you: if you begin on Midwinter's day (21st December) then that will be your first omen day that speaks about the month of January, and 22nd December will be your second omen day talking about February and so on. If you decide to use the traditional days of Christmas, then your first omen day is 26th December and speaks of January, with the rest following suit.

On each of the days, your question is going to be a request along the lines of 'Spirits of Nature, please give me an omen for the month of March,' or 'Guides and Guardians, please reveal what June will hold for me and my family/community.' The framing is very important or what you experience will have no root.

Your augury might be experienced during a daily walk, or perceived in the nature of the day itself and how it falls out at work or at home. Make a frame for each Omen Day by asking to be shown an augury from nature and allowing the next thing you experience, see or hear to be the sign you are expecting. It helps to find the right place to do this on a walk, where you can enter stillness, close your eyes and frame your question. Then spin around on the spot—in order to randomize what is experienced—and then open your eyes and be attentive to the first things you see or hear.

Pressed for Time

However, there will be days when even a quick walk isn't possible. In such cases you might just step out into your garden, enter stillness, frame your question and then turn slowly on the spot until you feel you are ready. Open your eyes and ears—you might see your neighbour hanging out the washing, a robin landing on a rose tree or hear the sudden acceleration of a car. In that moment, attend and listen to whatever has happened. Let's say you've asked about next August and when you open your eyes a flock of seagulls wheels overhead. The kinds of birds might be important, but then so is the way they are flying. In that moment, you might feel that August will have a new direction to it, that you will take a trip in the direction of their flight. These are the things you should write down on going back inside. You should also note how you felt when you experienced the omen.

Making Sense of It

Try to get out of your head and into your body when considering the experience you've had. You might consider the following:

- How are my question and my experience of the omen related?
- How did I feel when I saw/heard it?
- What sensations or memories did I experience?

Always take the first thing you experience as your omen and don't edit, amend or improve! On first taking omens, beginners inevitably second-guess what they see or hear by editing out the very first thing because 'it isn't what I want to see/hear.' On one notable occasion, imagine a student ignored a newspaper page blowing along the pavement, Even though it was the first thing she saw, in her eyes 'it was just rubbish.' However, the newspaper page had a big headline on the front that said 'No!' This may literally be the answer to the student's question about a decision she had to face.

Avoid any psychologizing of what you experience. This happens when your knowledge becomes an active agent—the receiving of omens is more physical and instinctual. If you see a white feather on the path before you, please just experience it as the answer to your question without going into a head trip about 'oh, white feathers mean cowardice, so my answer is....' Let the white feather just be itself: a wonderful gift from the universe that is speaking to you now. Pick it up and experience what happens when you hold the question in your heart—it will answer you!

Keeping a Record

Record your findings however faint, trivial or off-hand you think they are.

This is where the art of the omen will reveal itself to you, but you will have to be patient. Keep your findings safe where you can consult them again as the months unfold. Check your findings—they are often so exact it is breath-taking.

Augury is really the art of listening and attending to the universe, which has come to this one small point of attention to help answer your question.

The Omen Days give information in a variety of ways and are very adaptable to your circumstances. Even if you were bedridden or imprisoned in one room, you could still do it every day and discover different auguries. There is no right way to do this, only by the unique interaction you have between the world that is seen and the world that is unseen but just as real.

Whatever your beliefs, the Omen Days continue to offer the opportunity to understand the year ahead. So as the new year draws near, forget the 'year's round up of news' on the television this holiday and look ahead to a year full of promise that you alone have foreseen this midwinter!

—CAITLÍN MATTHEWS

MOON GARDENING

BY PHASE

Sow, transplant, bud and graft   *Plow, cultivate, weed and reap*

NEW	First Quarter	FULL	Last Quarter	NEW
Plant above-ground crops with outside seeds, flowering annuals.	Plant above-ground crops with inside seeds.	Plant root crops, bulbs, biennials, perennials.		Do not plant.

BY PLACE IN THE ZODIAC

In general—plant and transplant crops that bear above ground when the Moon is in a watery sign: Cancer, Scorpio or Pisces. Plant and transplant root crops when the Moon is in Taurus or Capricorn; the other earthy sign, Virgo, encourages rot. The airy signs, Gemini, Libra and Aquarius, are good for some crops and not for others. The fiery signs, Aries, Leo and Sagittarius, are barren signs for most crops and best used for weeding, pest control and cultivating the soil.

♈

Aries—*barren, hot and dry*. Favorable for planting and transplanting beets, onions and garlic, but unfavorable for all other crops. Good for weeding and pest control, for canning and preserving, and for all activities involving fire.

♉

Taurus—*fruitful, cold and dry*. Fertile, best for planting root crops and also very favorable for all transplanting as it encourages root growth. Good for planting crops that bear above ground and for canning and preserving. Prune in this sign to encourage root growth.

♊

Gemini—*barren, hot and moist*. The best sign for planting beans, which will bear more heavily. Unfavorable for other crops. Good for harvesting and for gathering herbs.

♋

Cancer—*fruitful, cold and moist*. Best for planting crops that bear above ground and very favorable for root crops. Dig garden beds when the Moon is in this sign, and everything planted in them will flourish. Prune in this sign to encourage growth.

♌

Leo—Nothing should be planted or transplanted while the Moon is in the Lion. Favorable for weeding and pest control, for tilling and cultivating the soil, and for canning and preserving.

♍

Virgo—*barren, cold and dry*. Good for planting grasses and grains, but unfavorable for other crops. Unfavorable for canning and preserving, but favorable for weeding, pest control, tilling and cultivating. Make compost when the Moon is in the Virgin and it will ripen faster.

♎︎

Libra—*fruitful, hot and moist*. The best sign to plant flowers and vines and somewhat favorable for crops that bear above the ground. Prune in this sign to encourage flowering.

♏︎

Scorpio—*fruitful, cold and moist*. Very favorable to plant and transplant crops that bear above ground, and favorable for planting and transplanting root crops. Set out fruit trees when the Moon is in this sign and prune to encourage growth.

♐︎

Sagittarius—*barren, hot and dry*. Favorable for planting onions, garlic and cucumbers, but unfavorable for all other crops, and especially unfavorable for transplanting. Favorable for canning and preserving, for tilling and cultivating the soil, and for pruning to discourage growth.

♑︎

Capricorn—*fruitful, cold and dry*. Very favorable for planting and transplanting root crops, favorable for flowers, vines, and all crops that bear above ground. Plant trees, bushes and vines in this sign. Prune trees and vines to strengthen the branches.

♒︎

Aquarius—*barren, hot and moist*. Favorable for weeding and pest control, tilling and cultivating the soil, harvesting crops, and gathering herbs. Somewhat favorable for planting crops that bear above ground, but only in dry weather or the seeds will tend to rot.

♓︎

Pisces—*fruitful, cold and moist*. Very favorable for planting and transplanting crops that bear above ground and favorable for flowers and all root crops except potatoes. Prune when the Moon is in the Fishes to encourage growth. Plant trees, bushes and vines in this sign.

Consult our Moon Calendar pages for phase and place in the zodiac circle. The Moon remains in a sign for about two and a half days. Match your gardening activity to the day that follows the Moon's entry into that zodiacal sign. For best results, choose days when the phase and sign are both favorable. For example, plant seeds when the Moon is waxing in a suitable fruitful sign, and uproot stubborn weeds when the Moon is in the fourth quarter in a barren sign.

Moon Gardening, a regular feature of the *The Witches' Almanac*, has been expanded this year to give further insight into the relationship between the Earth and the Moon. This enhancement was provided by John Michael Greer.

The MOON Calendar

is divided into zodiac signs rather than the more familiar Gregorian calendar.

2018   **2019**

Bear in mind that new projects should be initiated when the Moon is waxing (from dark to full). When the Moon is on the wane (from full to dark), it is a time for storing energy and the wise person waits.

Please note that Moons are listed by day of entry into each sign. Quarters are marked, but as rising and setting times vary from one region to another, it is advisable to check your local newspaper, library or planetarium.
The Moon's Place is computed for Eastern Time.

capricorn

December 21 2017 – January 19, 2018

Cardinal Sign of Earth ♁ *Ruled by Saturn* ♄

S	M	T	W	T	F	S
				Dec. **21** Winter Solstice ❄ Aquarius	**22** *Kiss the mistletoe*	**23** Pisces
24 *Listen to your familiar*	**25**	**26** Aries	**27** *Set a fire of oak*	**28** Taurus	**29**	**30** Gemini
31 *Summon Jack Frost*	Jan. **1** Wolf Moon Cancer	**2** WANING	**3** Leo	**4** *Family day*	**5** Virgo	**6** *Stir the cauldron*
7 Libra	**8**	**9** *Hold hands with your love*	**10** Scorpio	**11** *Weather the storm*	**12** Sagittarius	**13** *Look to the North*
14 *Build a snowman*	**15** Capricorn	**16**	**17** WAXING Aquarius	**18**	**19** *Make a wish*	

Water of Well-Being Go to the seashore after the tide turns from ebb to flood. Collect from the ninth wave a jar of sea water. The count begins at your discretion. It can be the first wave to touch your feet or a breaking crest you see at a distance. Counting the waves by sight is often confused by contrary currents or eddies, so it is far easier to close your eyes and depend on the sound of each wave as it hits the shore. Scoop up water from the ninth wave in one fluid motion.

– THE WITCHES' ALMANAC, *Love Charms*

土
狗

YEAR OF THE EARTH DOG
February 16, 2018–February 4, 2019

THE CHINESE ZODIAC is thought to be the oldest and most widely circulated of the world's zodiac calendars. In use for over 4,000 years throughout China, Japan, Korea, Cambodia and other countries in the Far East, it has migrated to the West and is as popular as ever. This zodiac follows a cycle of twelve years and incorporates five elements: fire, water, wood, metal and earth. Every sixty years the element-animal pairs repeat. The years are named in honor of the twelve animals who were rewarded by Buddha. Tradition says that Buddha awarded a year to each animal for responding to an invitation to attend his birthday party. They are forever the animals that hide in the hearts of each year. Based on a lunar calendar, the Chinese New Year begins with the second New Moon following the Winter Solstice. This date varies from year to year and takes place from late January to mid-February.

This is the Year of the Earth Dog. It promises to generate a universal urge to make the world a better place. A spirit of reform and vigilance prevails. Inequities in the world are noted and solutions are sought. Keeping promises, seeking knowledge and truth, service and all well meaning actions are the values upheld by this modest and sincere Brown Dog.

A devoted friend, faithful and honest, those born in a Dog year are trustworthy but will be dogmatic about upholding their own codes of ethics. A touch of rigidity combines with great sensitivity and anxiety. It takes time for a Dog to overcome vague worries. To those who don't understand them, Dogs can appear negative. In reality they are creative and constructive. Dogs do much good in the world and prefer to be physically active.

More information on the Earth Dog can be found on our website at
http://TheWitchesAlmanac.com/AlmanacExtras/.

Years of the Dog
1934, 1946, 1958, 1970, 1982, 1994, 2006, 2018, 2030

Illustration by Ogmios MacMerlin

aquarius

January 21 – February 18, 2018

Fixed Sign of Air ♎ Ruled by Uranus ♅

S	M	T	W	T	F	S

Diana of Ephesus Evolved from a date-palm tree sacred to the Amazons, the well-known statue of Diana is decorated with a festoon of ripe dates. Historical sources mistakenly identify the dates as breasts and dismiss the primary significance of the figure. The statue is a tribute to the tender regard held by Diana for both wild and domestic creatures. From waist to feet are carvings of rows of animals—lions, rams, bulls and deer. Cats climb to her shoulders and an ancient reference   CONTINUED BELOW

Jan. 20

Pisces

21 Write a letter	**22** Aries	**23**	**24** ◐ Taurus	**25**	**26** *Drop the sail* Gemini	**27**
28 Ring a bell Cancer	**29**	**30** Total Lunar Eclipse Blue Moon ⇨	**31** Storm Moon Leo	**Feb. 1** WANING Oimelc Eve	**2** Candlemas Virgo	**3** The kiss fades
4 Read tea leaves Libra	**5**	**6** Bewitch a stranger Scorpio	**7** ◑	**8** Sagittarius	**9** Burn a candle for love	**10**
11 Capricorn	**12**	**13** A love found Aquarius	**14** Lupercalia Partial Solar Eclipse ⇨	**15** ●	**16** Chinese New Year Earth Dog Pisces	**17** WAXING

18

notes the crab engraved on her breast, "a creature sacred to her." Upon the original statue, the one destroyed by a Christian zealot in A.D. 400, a mysterious inscription appeared in three places: at her feet, girdle and crown. ASKI. KATASKI. HAIX. TETRAZ. DAMNAMENEUS. AISION translated as follows: Darkness-Light-Himself-The Sun-Truth.

– Elizabeth Pepper, *Moon Lore*

Aries

The Virgin on the Crescent
Albrecht Dürer

♓ pisces

February 19 – March 20, 2018

Mutable Sign of Water ▽ Ruled by Neptune ♆

S	M	T	W	T	F	S
	Feb. 19 Start early	20	21 Break the ice Taurus	22	23 ◑ Gemini	24
25 Bide your time Cancer	26	27 Remove an obstacle Leo	28 Matronalia ⇨	Mar. 1 Chaste Moon Virgo	2 WANING	3 Renounce bigotry Libra
4 Call an old friend	5 Scorpio	6	7 Intensify efforts	8 Sagittarius	9 ◐	10 Capricorn
11 Lighten your burden	12	13 Enjoy whimsy Aquarius	14 Put your house in order	15 Pisces	16 Wake the earth	17 ● Aries
18 WAXING	19 Minerva's Day	20 Taurus				

Rhodonite A pink stone with black veining, usually found as a massive single stone; sometimes smaller crystals are found, rare and more valuable. The name "rhodonite" is derived from the Greek "rhodon," meaning "rose." Typically this stone is found in Europe and Australia, but sometimes emerges elsewhere in the world.

Rhodonite is a stone of love and often this sentiment is manifest in self actualization. The earthly gem helps to stabilize emotions, which provides confidence and allows wearers to achieve their full potential. Often helpful in friendships, relationships and negotiating, rhodonite would do well placed in a desk drawer or near the threshold of your front door.

— ELIZABETH PEPPER, *The ABC of Magic Charms*

To Be a Pilgrim

The Canterbury Tales are stories told by pilgrims meeting on the road to the cathedral dedicated to Sir Thomas Becket. In the book, the "frame story" is set up by the poetic prologue, the following a modern English excerpt. The marvelous tales are allegedly from a story-telling contest by the medieval pilgrims as they await daylight at an inn. The author once received a free dinner for winning a story-telling contest.

> *In Southwark, at the Tabard, as I lay*
> *Ready to start upon my pilgrimage*
> *To Canterbury, full of devout homage,*
> *There came at nightfall to that hostelry*
> *Some nine and twenty in a company*
> *Of sundry persons who had chanced to fall*
> *In fellowship, and pilgrims were they all*
> *That toward Canterbury town would ride.*
> *The rooms and stables spacious were and wide,*
> *And well we there were eased, and of the best.*
> *And briefly, when the sun had gone to rest,*
> *So had I spoken with them, every one,*
> *That I was of their fellowship anon,*
> *And made agreement that we'd early rise*
> *To take the road, as you I will apprise.*
>
> Geoffrey Chaucer (1342-1400),
> *The Canterbury Tales,* General Prologue excerpt

To see the original Middle English version of the lines, check out our Web site at www.TheWitchesAlmanac.com. A fascinating way to view how our language has evolved.

CHAUCERS CANTERBURY PILGRIMS

aries

March 20 – April 19, 2018

Cardinal Sign of Fire △ Ruled by Mars ♂

S	M	T	W	T	F	S
		Mar **20** Vernal Equinox Taurus	**21**	**22** Make a change Gemini	**23**	**24** Cancer
25	**26** Feel passion within Leo	**27**	**28** Know your boundaries Virgo	**29**	**30** Libra	**31** Seed Moon
April **1** WANING April Fools Day	**2** Scorpio	**3**	**4** Dance! Sagittarius	**5**	**6** Start a new venture Capricorn	**7**
8 Aquarius	**9**	**10**	**11** Drink sacred water Pisces	**12**	**13** Show love	**14** Aries
15	**16** WAXING Taurus	**17**	**18** Contact friends Gemini	**19**		

MUSTARD: The seed taken either by itself, or with other things, either in an electuary or drink, doth mightily stir up bodily lust, and helps the spleen and pains in the sides, and gnawings in the bowels; and used as a gargle draws up the palate of the mouth, being fallen down; and also it dissolves the swellings about the throat, if it be outwardly applied.—*The Complete Herbal* by Nicholas Culpeper

TAROT'S STRENGTH

THE ENCHANTRESS. THE CHARMER. THE WITCH. Once known as the Lady of the Beasts, Goddess of the Cosmic Lion, the Queen of the Animals. She dominates the creatures of the animal world but does not fight them; between them there is no hostility or antagonism. She rules over the unconscious powers that take animal form in our dreams. She handles that which prowls and howls just outside the safe walls of culture and consciousness.

Strength knows that all the impulse and anxiety of the individual and the community must ultimately be subordinated to the life and purpose of the species. It is the spiritual order of the whole that appears as the Lady of the Beasts. She is the strength and vitality of the life force that manifests through the feminine, whose ultimate purpose is the continuation of the species, who represents love without division, love without judgement. She is the power of love to tame the inhuman forces of life through her gentle touch and the direct physical contact of human relationships.

Strength gives us fortitude, the energy for work and creativity, the desire to exert ourselves with a force beyond the reach of the conscious mind. Strength is our basic survival mechanism, whether as anger or rage rebelling against whatever threatens life, or as lust leading to the regeneration of the species or the expression of our own creativity. The strongest power in the world is love. Just as we can conquer all through love, we must learn to love all parts of our nature—the bestial and the divine.

taurus
April 20 – May 20, 2018
Fixed Sign of Earth ▽ Ruled by Venus ♀

S	M	T	W	T	F	S
LOVAGE: It is an herb of the Sun, under the sign Taurus. If Saturn offend the throat (as he always doth if he be occasioner of the malady, and in[109] Taurus is the Genesis) this is your cure. It opens, cures and digests humours, and mightily provokes women's courses and urine. CONTINUED BELOW					April **20** Cancer	**21**
22 ◑ Leo	**23** *Don't be stubborn*	**24**	**25** *Avoid decay* Virgo	**26**	**27** *Plant first seeds* Libra	**28**
29 (Hare Moon) Scorpio	**30** WANING *Walpurgis Night*	May **1** Beltane Sagittarius	**2** *Dance the Maypole* ⇐	**3**	**4** Capricorn	**5**
6 Aquarius	**7** ◑	**8** White Lotus Day	**9** *Read to the bees* Pisces	**10**	**11** Aries	**12**
13 Taurus	**14** *Blow a kiss to the Moon*	**15** ●	**16** WAXING Gemini	**17** *A windy day*	**18** Cancer	**19**
20 Leo	Half a dram at a time of the dried root in powder taken in wine, doth wonderfully warm a cold stomach, helps digestion, and consumes all raw and superfluous moisture therein; eases all inward gripings and pains, dissolves wind, and resists poison and infection. —*The Complete Herbal* by Nicholas Culpeper					

Notable Quotations
PLANTS

Where you tend a rose, my lad
A thistle cannot grow.
Frances Hodgson Burnett

The Earth laughs in flowers.
Ralph Waldo Emerson

If you have a sapling in your hand and someone tells you the Messiah has arrived, first plant the sapling.
Rabbi Yochanan ben Zakkai

There are always flowers for those who want to see them.
Henri Matisse

Let us learn to appreciate there will be times when the trees will be bare, and look forward to the time when we may pick the fruit.
Anton Chekhov

The true meaning of life is to plant trees, under whose shade you do not expect to sit.
Nelson Henderson

As for the garden of mint, the very smell of it alone recovers and refreshes our spirits, as the taste stirs up our appetite for meat.
Pliny the Elder

My heart is like an apple-tree whose boughs are bent with thickset fruit.
Christina Rossetti

The temple bell stops but I still hear the sound coming out of the flowers.
Matsuo Basho

Miss Ainslie gathered a bit of rosemary, crushing it between her white fingers. "See," she said, "some of us are like that—it takes a blow to find the sweetness in our souls."
Lavender and Old Lace
Myrtle Reed (1874–1911)
American Poet and Journalist

Quotes compiled by Isabel Kunkle.

gemini
May 21 – June 20, 2018
Mutable Sign of Air △ Ruled by Mercury ☿

S	M	T	W	T	F	S
	May **21**	**22**	**23** Read a book	**24**	**25** Watch the Birds	**26**
		Virgo		Libra		Scorpio
27	**28** Oak Apple Day ⇨	**29** Dyad Moon	**30** WANING Vesak Day ⇦	**31**	June **1** Cast a love spell	**2**
		Sagittarius		Capricorn		
3	**4** Call an old friend	**5** Night of the Watchers	**6**	**7**	**8**	**9**
Aquarius		Pisces			Aries	
10 Enjoy solitude	**11**	**12**	**13**	**14** WAXING	**15** Wisdom is heard	**16**
Taurus		Gemini		Cancer		Leo
17	**18**	**19** Offer to the Faries	**20**			
	Virgo		Libra			

FERN: It is under the dominion of Mercury, both male and female. The roots of both these sorts of Fern being bruised and boiled in mead, or honeyed water, and drank, kills the broad and long worms in the body, and abates the swelling and hardness of the spleen. The green leaves eaten, purge the belly of choleric and waterish humours that trouble the stomach. They are dangerous for women with child to meddle with, by reason they cause abortions.—*The Complete Herbal* by Nicholas Culpeper

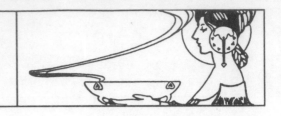

KITCHEN MAGIC

Applesauce

APPLESAUCE, SO BASIC, so comforting, so good. Apples are steeped in lore and tradition and found worldwide. They are nourishing, healthful and magical. Apples are associated with love, healing, beauty, wisdom and divination, finding their way into myths, fairytales and cultural stories. No matter how they are eaten—just picked and out of hand, jellied, spiced or dried—from late summer into winter and preserved they see us through the entire year.

Apples are feminine in nature, associated with the planet Venus and the element water. If an apple is cut widthwise a five-pointed star appears in both halves. These symbols, as well as the seeds are used for divination. To ensure fidelity share one with your lover. Apple blossoms are used in love and healing incense. Wands made from apple wood are very magical. Apples are important at Samhain—a symbol of immortality—and are often gifted to the dead to feed the souls traveling on Hallows night. At Midwinter "wassail" your orchards and gardens to ensure abundance in the next growing season. And best of all, share the Wassail Bowl with kith and kin during the winter holidays.

Applesauce, especially served warm, compliments any holiday meal. It is comforting and healing when you are under the weather.

Making Applesauce

6 apples - 2 Golden Delicious, 2 Granny Smith and 2 Jonagold (at some farmers markets you can purchase a bag of apples that are combined especially to make good sauce or pie)

water

sugar (optional)

pinch of salt

spices, to taste (cinnamon, nutmeg, ginger, cardamom, mace, clove)

1-2 Tsp butter or cream (my secret ingredient – gives the sauce a little richness)

Cut, peel and core the apples. For a rustic sauce leave the peel on. If you would like a pink tinge to your sauce cook with some of the red peel from the Jonagolds. Place in a large sauce pan with just enough water to keep the apples from scorching. The natural sugar in the apples will burn without water but you do not want too much, making it soppy. Simmer until the apples start to soften and cook through. Cool slightly. Using a potato masher smash the apples to desired consistency (fine or chunky). Add remaining ingredients to your taste.

—BRIGID NEEDFIRE

cancer

June 21 – July 22, 2018

Cardinal Sign of Water ▽ *Ruled by Moon* ☽

S	M	T	W	T	F	S
WILD CLARY: It is something hotter and drier than the garden Clary is, yet nevertheless under the dominion of the Moon, as well as that; the seeds of it being beat to powder, and drank with wine, is an admirable help to provoke lust. A decoction of the leaves CONTINUED BELOW				June **21** Summer Solstice ☼	**22** *Gather St. John's Wort*	**23** Scorpio
24 Midsummer	**25** Sagittarius	**26**	**27** *Summon the Moon*	**28** Mead Moon Capricorn	**29** WANING	**30** *Embrace your familiars* Aquarius
July **1** *Carry three pebbles*	**2** Pisces	**3** *Avoid thorns*	**4**	**5** Aries	**6**	**7** Taurus
8	**9** Gemini	**10** *Toss water into the air*	**11** *Read* Cancer	**12**	**13** Partial Solar Eclipse ⇐	**14** WAXING Leo
15	**16**	**17** *Stay clear of fire* Virgo	**18** Libra	**19**	**20** *Isis calls* Scorpio	**21**
22 Sagitarrius	being drank, warms the stomach, and it is a wonder if it should not, the stomach being under Cancer, the house of the Moon.—*The Complete Herbal* by Nicholas Culpeper					

 # TALISMAN

The Sator Square

```
S A T O R
A R E P O
T E N E T
O P E R A
R O T A S
```

THE USE OF THE SATOR Square as a talisman of defense is buried in the annals of time, its origins being lost to antiquity. With the individual words of the Latin sentence SATOR AREPO TENET OPERA ROTAS each arranged to ccupy a single row of the square, an interesting phenomenon is observed. As you can see in the above illustration the text can be read top-to-bottom, bottom-to-top, left-to-right or right-to-left. Additionally it can be rotated 180 degrees with the results yielding the same word order.

The individual translations of the words shed some light on the meaning behind this talisman; Sator can be translated as "the founder or a divine progenitor." The meaning of word Arepo is a bit unclear, as it may simply be a proper noun or a shortening of the Latin word arrepo, meaning "to creep towards." Tenet is translated by some as "to have mastery over." Opera means "to work." Lastly Rotas meaning "wheel or rotating." A possible translation of the entire sentence being: The Great Sower holds in his hand all works.

Written in the Ink of Arte (such as dragon's blood or ink with other herbs), this talisman is a potent protection of the threshold not only of your home, but your magical working area.

The square can also be used as a focal point for astral journey during meditation.
—DEVON STRONG

leo

July 23 – August 22, 2018
Fixed Sign of Fire △ Ruled by Sun ☉

S	M	T	W	T	F	S
	July **23** Ancient Egyptian New Year	**24** *Eat parsley*	**25** Capricorn	**26** *Celebrate Esbat*	**27** Wort Moon Aquarius	**28** Total Lunar Eclipse ⇦ WANING
29 *Cook corn*	**30**. Pisces	**31** Lughnassad Eve Aries	Aug. **1** Lammas	**2** *Bake bread*	**3** Taurus	**4**
5 *Don't burn*	**6** Gemini	**7**	**8** *Hear the drums* Cancer	**9**	**10** Partial Solar Eclipse ⇨ Leo	**11**
12 WAXING Virgo	**13** Diana's Day *Taste lemon*	**14** *Make an incense* Libra	**15**	**16** Black Cat Appreciation Day Scorpio	**17**	**18** Sagittarius
19 *Enjoy friends company*	**20**	**21** Capricorn	**22**			

ANGELICA: It is an herb of the Sun in Leo; let it be gathered when he is there, the Moon applying to his good aspect; let it be gathered either in his hour, or in the hour of Jupiter, let Sol be angular; observe the like in gathering the herbs of other planets, and you may happen to do wonders. In all epidemical diseases caused by Saturn, that is as good a preservative as grows: It resists poison, by defending and comforting the heart, blood, and spirits; it doth the like against the plague and all epidemical diseases, if the root be taken in powder to the weight of half a dram at a time.—*The Complete Herbal* by Nicholas Culpeper

Ivy

Gort

WHEN IVY TRAILS along the ground it remains weak and does not produce fruit, but when it climbs using a tree or a wall for support, it grows increasingly stronger putting out flowers in autumn and berries in the spring. Birds feast on ivy's purple-black berries, scattering the seeds to form new plants in the soft spring earth. Ivy draws no nourishment from the tree it climbs nor do its underground roots seriously compete with the tree's root for nutrients in the soil. Ivy growing up the walls of buildings promotes dryness within and serves as a protective shield against the atmosphere. Its botanical name in Latin is *Hedera helix* and describes ivy's spiral form of growth, helix means "to turn round."

The rich deep evergreen color and climbing spiral action inspired the ancients to identify ivy with immortality, resurrection and rebirth. The classical gods of wine, the Greek Dionysos and his Roman counterpart Bacchus, are often depicted wearing crowns of ivy. The association with the grapevine, which also grows in spiral form, gave ivy the reputation for diminishing drunkenness, for it was thought that one spiral reversed the power of the other. Ivy came to symbolize fidelity and one perfect leaf collected when the Moon was one day old was a useful amulet in matters of love.

virgo

August 23 – September 22, 2018

Mutable Sign of Earth ▽ Ruled by Mercury ☿

S	M	T	W	T	F	S
				Aug. **23**	**24**	**25**
				Aquarius		
26 Barley Moon — Pisces	**27** WANING	**28** *Avoid strong spices* — Aries	**29**	**30**	**31** *Know solitude* — Taurus	Sept. **1** *Promote peace*
2 — Gemini	**3**	**4** *Taste honey* — Cancer	**5**	**6** *6 times 6* — Leo	**7**	**8** *Visit the sick* — Virgo
9	**10** WAXING — Libra	**11** *Offer milk*	**12** Scorpio	**13** Ganesh Festival — *Dodge a hex*	**14**	**15** Sagittarius
16	**17** — Capricorn	**18** *Gather grain*	**19**	**20** *Change your luck* — Aquarius	**21**	**22** Autumnal Equinox ♌ Pisces

FENNEL: One good old fashion is not yet left off, viz. to boil Fennel with fish; for it consumes that phlegmatic humour, which fish most plentifully afford and annoy the body with, though few that use it know wherefore they do it; I suppose the reason of its benefit this way is because it is an herb of Mercury, and under Virgo, and therefore bears antipathy to Pisces. Fennel is good to break wind, to provoke urine, and ease the pains of the stone, and helps to break it. —*The Complete Herbal* by Nicholas Culpeper

A Zen Master's Everyday Guide

Soyen Shaku, the first Zen teacher to come to America, said , "My heart burns like fire but my eyes are as cold as dead ashes." He made the following rules which he practiced every day of his life:

In the morning before dressing, light incense and meditate.

Retire at a regular hour. Partake of food at regular intervals. Eat with moderation and never to the point of satisfaction.

Receive a guest with the same attitude you have when alone. When alone, maintain the same attitude you have in receiving guests.

Watch what you say, and whatever you say, practice it.

When an opportunity comes do not let it pass you by, yet always think twice before acting.

Do not regret the past. Look to the future.

Have the fearless attitude of a hero and the loving heart of a child.

Upon retiring, sleep as if you had entered your last sleep. Upon awakening, leave your bed behind you instantly as if you had cast away a pair of old shoes.

libra

September 23 – October 22, 2018

Cardinal Sign of Air △ Ruled by Venus ♀

LIBRA

S	M	T	W	T	F	S
Sept. **23**	**24** Blood Moon Aries	**25** WANING	**26** *Take heed*	**27** Taurus	**28**	**29** *Tavel safely* Gemini
30	Oct. **1** *Do magick* Cancer	**2**	**3**	**4** *Create* Leo	**5**	**6** Virgo
7 *Snakes hide*	**8** Libra	**9** WAXING	**10** *Catch a falling leaf* Scorpio	**11** *Make a wish*	**12** *Feed the birds* Sagittarrius	**13**
14	**15** Capricorn	**16**	**17** *Feed the birds again* Aquarius	**18**	**19** *Share a cup of tea*	**20** Pisces
21	**22** Aries					

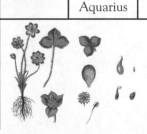

KIDNEYWORT: Venus challenges the herb under Libra. The juice or the distilled water being drank, is very effectual for all inflammations and unnatural heats, to cool a fainting hot stomach, a hot liver, or the bowels: the herb, juice, or distilled water thereof, outwardly applied, heals pimples, St. Anthony's fire, and other outward heats. The said juice or water helps to heal sore kidneys, torn or fretted by the stone, or exulcerated within; it also provokes urine, is available for the dropsy, and helps to break the stone. Being used as a bath, or made into an ointment, it cools the painful piles or hæmorrhoidal veins.—*The Complete Herbal* by Nicholas Culpeper

The Red Queen lecturing Alice, by John Tenniel
Through the Looking Glass and what Alice found there

scorpio

October 23 – November 21, 2018

Fixed Sign of Water ▽ Ruled by Pluto ♇

♏ SCORPIVS

S	M	T	W	T	F	S
		Oct. **23**	**24** Snow Moon Taurus	**25** WANING	**26** *Know pleasure*	**27** Gemini
28	**29** Cancer	**30** *Samhain Eve* ⇨	**31** Leo	Nov. **1** Hallowmas	**2** Virgo	**3** *Cast chains and bones*
4 *Honor ancestors* Libra	**5**	**6** *Ghosts are hungry. Beware!* Scorpio	**7**	**8** WAXING	**9** *Paint something red* Sagittarius	**10**
11 Capricorn	**12**	**13** Aquarius	**14** *Read the Tarot*	**15**	**16** Hecate Night Pisces	**17**
18 *Burn old corn stalks* Aries	**19**	**20** *Light the cauldron*	**21** Taurus			

PLANTAIN: It is true, Misaldus and others, yea, almost all astrology-physicians, hold this to be an herb of Mars, because it cures the diseases of the head and privities, which are under the houses of Mars, Aries, and Scorpio: The truth is, it is under the command of Venus, and cures the head by antipathy to Mars, and the privities by sympathy to Venus; neither is there hardly a martial disease but it cures.—*The Complete Herbal* by Nicholas Culpeper

THE RELIGION OF THE FUTURE will be a cosmic religion. It should transcend a personal God and avoid dogmas and theology. Covering both the natural and the spiritual, it should be based on a religious sense arising from the experience of all things, natural and spiritual and a meaningful unity. Buddhism answers this description. If there is any religion that would cope with modern scientific needs, it would be Buddhism.

ALBERT EINSTEIN

sagittarius

November 22 – December 20, 2018

Mutable Sign of Fire △ Ruled by Jupiter ♃

S	M	T	W	T	F	S
				Nov. **22** Draw down the Moon	**23** ◯ Gemini	**24** WANING
25 Cancer	**26**	**27** Be playful Leo	**28**	**29** ◑ Virgo	**30**	Dec. **1** Libra
2	**3**	**4** Rest Scorpio	**5**	**6** Reflect Sagittarius	**7** ⬤	**8** WAXING Capricorn
9 Hold freinds dear	**10**	**11** Win the race Aquarius	**12**	**13** Pisces	**14** Visit the ocean	**15** ◑
16 Fairy Queen Eve Aries	**17** Saturnalia	**18** Taurus	**19** Annoint a charm	**20** Gemini		

SAGE: Jupiter claims this, and bids me tell you, it is good for the liver, and to breed blood. A decoction of the leaves and branches of Sage made and drank, saith Dioscorides, provokes urine, brings down women's courses, helps to expel the dead child, and causes hair to become black. It stays the bleeding of wounds, and cleanses foul ulcers. Three spoonfuls of the juice of Sage taken fasting, with a little honey, doth presently stay the spitting or casting of blood of them that are in a consumption.—*The Complete Herbal* by Nicholas Culpeper

The North Wind and the Sun

THE NORTH WIND and the Sun disputed as to which was the most powerful, and agreed that he who could first strip a wayfaring man of his clothes should be declared the victor. The North Wind first tried his power and blew with all his might, but the keener his blasts the closer the Traveler wrapped his cloak around him, until at last, resigning all hope of victory, the Wind called upon the Sun to see what he could do. The Sun suddenly shone out with all his warmth. The Traveler no sooner felt his genial rays than he took off one garment after another. At last, fairly overcome with heat. He undressed and bathed in a stream that lay in his path.

Moral: Persuasion is better than Force.

capricorn

December 21 2018 – January 19, 2019

Cardinal Sign of Earth ♄ Ruled by Saturn ♄

S	M	T	W	T	F	S
COMFREY: This is an herb of Saturn, and I suppose under the sign Capricorn, cold, dry, and earthy in quality. What was spoken of Clown's Woundwort may be said of this. The Great Comfrey helps those that spit blood, or make a bloody urine. The root CONTINUED BELOW					Dec. **21** Winter Solstice ❄	**22** Wolf Moon Cancer
23 WANING	**24** Leo	**25**	**26** Clean the house Virgo	**27**	**28**	**29** ◑ Libra
30.	**31** Be flexible Scorpio	Jan. **1**	**2** Cleanse the house Sagittarius	**3**	**4** Partial Solar Eclipse ⇨	**5** ● Capricorn
6 WAXING	**7** Have hope Aquarius	**8**	**9** Feast of Janus Know your limits	**10** Pisces	**11** Exaggerate a bit	**12** Aries
13	**14** ◐	**15** Express gratitude Taurus	**16**	**17** Gamble Gemini	**18**	**19** Cancer

The root boiled in water or wine, and the decoction drank, helps all inward hurts, bruises, wounds, and ulcer of the lungs, and causes the phlegm that oppresses them to be easily spit forth: It helps the defluction of rheum from the head upon the lungs, the fluxes of blood or humours by the belly, women's immoderate courses, as well the reds as the whites, and the running of the reins happening by what cause soever.—*The Complete Herbal* by Nicholas Culpeper

PROVERBS OF THE WORLD

*Short, sharp and often ironic, proverbs
enliven conversation everywhere.*

A drowning man is not troubled by rain. *Persian*

God could not be everywhere and therefore he made mothers. *Yiddish*

Every ass loves to hear himself bray. *Anonymous*

A hen is heavy when carried far. *Irish*

Do not look where you fell, but where you slipped. *African*

Do not use a hatchet to remove a fly from a friend's forehead. *Anonymous*

A closed mouth catches no flies. *Italian*

He lies like an eyewitness. *Russian insult*

Flattery makes friends and truth makes enemies. *Spanish*

A loan though old is not a gift. *Hungarian*

A rumor goes in one ear and out many mouths. *Chinese*

Call on God, but row away from the rocks. *Indian*

A thief believes everyone steals. *Anonymous*

Wonder is the beginning of wisdom. *Greek*

A hungry man is an angry man. *English*

When spider webs unite, they can tie up a lion. *Ethiopian*

In baiting a mousetrap with cheese, always leave room for the mouse. *Greek*

It is better to exist unknown to the law. *Irish*

Never marry for money. Ye'll borrow it cheaper. *Scottish*

One of these days is none of these days. *English*

Sit a beggar at your table and he will soon put his feet on it. *Russian*

War is death's feast. *Anonymous*

Want a thing long enough and you don't. *Chinese*

When the mouse laughs at the cat, there is a hole nearby. *Nigerian*

Young wood makes a hot fire. *Greek*

Better give a penny than lend twenty. *Italian*

 *The Irish way with words is legendary. A traditional
Irish curse—may it never fall on your own shell-like ears...*
May the curse of Mary Malone and her nine blind
illegitimate children chase you so far over the hills of
Damnation that the Lord himself can't find you with
a telescope.

aquarius

January 21 – February 18, 2019
Fixed Sign of Air ♎ Ruled by Uranus ♅

S	M	T	W	T	F	S
Jan. **20** Total Lunar Eclipse ⇨	**21** Storm Moon Leo	**22** WANING	**23** Virgo	**24**	**25** Libra	**26**
27 Scorpio	**28**	**29** *Contemplate silver wings* Sagittarius	**30**	**31**	Feb. **1** Oimelc Eve Capricorn	**2** Candlemas
3 *Sing to Diana* Aquarius	**4**	**5** Chinese New Year Earth Boar WAXING	**6** *Gaze into dark water* Pisces	**7**	**8** Aries	**9** *Help a friend*
10	**11** Taurus	**12**	**13** *Sing an enchantment* Gemini	**14**	**15** Acknowledge you love Lupercalia Cancer	**16** *Make wine*
17 Leo	**18** *Cast a Moon circle*					

BEETS: The government of these two sorts of Beets are far different; the red Beet being under Saturn and the[21] white under Jupiter; therefore take the virtues of them apart, each by itself. The white Beet much loosens the belly, and is of a cleansing, digesting quality, and provokes urine. The juice of it opens obstructions both of the liver and spleen, and is good for the head-ache and swimmings therein, and turnings of the brain; and is effectual also against all venomous creatures; and applied to the temples, stays inflammations of the eyes; it helps burnings, being used with oil, and with a little alum put to it, is good for St. Anthony's fire.—*The Complete Herbal* by Nicholas Culpeper

TYPHON

Monster father, monster children

FEW MONSTERS have children for obvious reasons—mates are not readily to be found, especially for an entity described as "grisly." So indeed was Typhon, who embodied volcanic forces. All we know about Echidna, his spouse, is that she was "hideous" and that the couple begat brutish children. Typhon had a hundred horrible dragon heads that wriggled upward to the stars, lava and red-hot stones poured from his gaping mouths, and venom dripped from his evil eyes. He embodied deep volcanic forces, and like other monsters was a foe of deities and heroes. From his hundred mouths, Typhon hissed and roared as he hurled sizzling mountains at the Gods, who fled in terror.

"The whole earth seethed, and sky and sea: and the long waves raged along the beaches around and about, at the rush of the deathless gods: and there arose an endless shaking," the Greek poet Hesiod reports.

Only Zeus stood his ground even as Mount Etna was hurled at him, and terrible combat raged. Zeus struck the mountain with a black cloud of thunderbolts and the mountain fell back on Typhon, pinning him below. And there the monster remains to this day, sinister as ever, belching fire and smoke and rage. But he is also otherwise immortal.

During the battle, Echidna cowered in a cave to protect the couple's offspring, resembling their parents in eerie ways: Cerberus, the three-headed watchdog guards the Gate of Hell; the Sphinx, a winged lion with the head and breasts of a woman, the "Demon of Death"; the Chimera breathes fire and has the disparate parts of a lion's head, goat's body and dragon's tail; the Hydra lives in a swamp, has a hundred heads which can regenerate; Ladon, a hundred-headed dragon guards the golden apple tree in the Garden of Hesperides; the vast Nemean lion has teeth and claws like swords.

Zeus came to destroy Echidna and her atrocious brood, but the mother begged for their lives. Zeus spared the creatures for the most amazing of reasons—because future Greek heroes needed worthy challengers. And the monster siblings were destroyed by the most powerful of heroes. Hercules, the son of Zeus, prevailed over the beasts during the course of his legendary Twelve Labors.

—BARBARA STACY

pisces

February 19 – March 20, 2019

Mutable Sign of Water ▽ Ruled by Neptune ♆

S	M	T	W	T	F	S
		Feb. **19** Chaste Moon Virgo	**20** WANING	**21** Libra	**22**	**23** Scorpio
24 Abandon chaos	**25**	**26** Sagittarius	**27** Walk straight	**28** Capricorn	Mar. **1** Matronalia	**2**
3 Aquarius	**4** Pray for light	**5** Pisces	**6** ●	**7** WAXING	**8** Aries	**9** Burn frankincense
10 Taurus	**11** Tell a secret	**12** Gemini	**13** Toss a coin	**14** Cancer	**15**	**16**
17 Leo	**18** Light a red candle	**19** Minerva's Day Virgo	**20** ○			

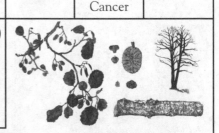

ALDER-TREE: It is a tree under the dominion of Venus, and of some watery sign or others, I suppose Pisces; and therefore the decoction, or distilled water of the leaves, is excellent against burnings and inflammations, either with wounds or without, to bathe the place grieved with, and especially for that inflammation in the breast, which the vulgar call an ague. —*The Complete Herbal* by Nicholas Culpeper

HALF HANGED MARY

The Witch of Hadley, Massachusetts

MARY (REEVE) WEBSTER was born in England in about 1624. At age 53 she married William Webster of Hadley, Massachusetts, a second son with few prospects. Mary and William were poor and the town was required to give them charity. According to reports, Mary had a temper which was probably made worse by her straightened circumstances. Given to harsh words she offended her neighbors who began to taunt her with the name "Witch."

It was said that cattle and horses being driven by her door would unaccountably stall. The driver would then enter her house and beat her, after which the animals would easily move forward. One time she entered a house and the baby within rose into the air and fell back three times from its cradle without anyone touching it. At another house a hen fell down the chimney and into the cooking pot where it was scalded. Soon afterwards Mary was found to be scalded also — clear evidence of Witchcraft.

On March 27, 1683 Mary was brought to the county court in Northampton. She was determined to have entered into a covenant and had familiarity with the Devil, while in the form of a fisher cat. It was said the Devil's imps would suck on her and that she had extra teats and marks on her body.

Mary was handed over for trial in Boston on May 22, 1683, where she pleaded "not guilty" and the jury evidently agreed because they sent her back home to Hadley. The village was not pleased with this and soon accusations began that she was bent upon revenge. According to Cotton Mather's *Magnalia*, Mary began to

72

attack a certain Philip Smith, aged fifty, who was a deacon of the church, a member of the general court, a justice in the county court, a selectman and a lieutenant of the troops.

Smith had set about "relieving the indigences" of a "wretched woman" in town who "expressed herself to him in such a manner" that he feared harm would come to him. In January 1684 Smith became ill and suspected that Mary had "made impressions with inchantments upon him."

Some young men of the village went to Mary's house to "give disturbance" to her and it was said that these were the only times Smith could finally fall asleep. Medicine was provided for Smith which "unaccountably emptied." Fire was seen on his bed which would vanish if any onlooker mentioned it and all around it scratching sounds were heard. Something as big as a cat was seen to move around in the bed and the bed would sometimes shake violently.

When Smith eventually succumbed, noises were heard in the room like a clattering of stools and chairs. Cotton Mather declared that Smith was "murdered with a hideous Witchcraft"

and when examined post mortem, Smith's body was found to be riddled with holes, as from awls.

Local boys took matters into their own hands while Smith was still alive and dragged Mary away from her house. There they hanged her by the neck and buried her in the snow, leaving her for dead. But she did not die. Mary lived another eleven years and went to her grave at about age 70 on June 3, 1698. She is buried in Old Hadley Cemetery in Hadley, Hampshire County, Massachusetts.

Mary was the fourth Hampshire County resident sent to Boston to be tried as a Witch. All four were acquitted and no Hampshire County person was ever executed for Witchcraft. Through the years, nine or ten Massachusetts and Connecticut residents were executed for Witchcraft and in 1692 twenty persons were killed in Salem Village due to a destructive and delusional Witch-hunting frenzy. The local people were so ashamed of what they had done that less than a year later the mania stopped and persecutions of Witches ended in New England.

—ELLEN EVERT HOPMAN

Baten Kaitos

The Topaz Light Burning In The Whale's Belly

Baten Kaitos, currently located at 21 degrees Aries 51 minutes, is the fixed star featured this year. Its importance was first noted in "Astronomica," an elegant masterpiece of science and scholarship written around the first century CE and attributed to Marcus Manilus, a legendary Roman poet and astrologer. Manilus wrote extensively, coherently and passionately about the Zodiac and the significance of the celestial influences. He deemed this small, yellowish-colored star important enough to devote almost the entire fifth and final book of his voluminous work to it. Baten Kaitos forms the belly of the constellation Cetus, the Whale. Manilus explains its influence through a mythological metaphor.

Baten Kaitos is connected to the legendary hero Perseus. It seems that a beautiful maiden, Andromeda, became a focus for the wrath of

Neptune. The trouble all started when Andromeda made Neptune's less attractive daughters, the Nereids, jealous. So the angry sea god sent a whale to kill her. Andromeda might even have been swallowed alive. Then Perseus arrived and killed the creature, saving the damsel in distress. A Mesopotamian legend involving the sinister sea serpent Tiamat and the biblical account of Jonah being rescued by God after being swallowed by a whale reflect this same theme. These stories are all symbolic descriptions of the importance of this fixed star. Its name translates from the Arabian Al Batn al Kaitos, meaning "from the whale's belly."

Baten Kaitos has the qualities of Mars and Saturn, according to Ptolemy, another early astrologer who wrote extensively about astrology's fixed stars. Warlike and emotional, it brings a glimpse of death. The possibility of perishing is followed by rescue and redemption. It also helps to recover lost goods and offers the benefits of experience gained following a time of crisis, especially if it is conjunct Mercury or Chiron. Being of good courage is essential in order to make the best of situations which are presented when this star is a factor in either an event chart or in the natal horoscope of an individual. Health-wise, Baten Kaitos has been linked to problems with balance and the ears. This is likely if it is conjunct Saturn. When favorable, in conjunction with Venus or Jupiter, it attracts acts of charity. Fickle, fated and vacillating, it underscores the temporary nature of victory and defeat. It points to transportation and travel. Obstacles of some kind are always present when this star is prominent in horoscopes. The release of the willpower and strength needed to overcome blockages and move to a higher plane offers a positive spin. Compulsory and uncomfortable change, shipwrecks, isolation, emigration and depression or loneliness are other keynotes. Use a very small orb of just two degrees from a conjunction with a luminary or personal planet when considering the influence of this distant yet potent star. Those born from April 10–14 of any year will have the Sun conjunct Baten Kaitos. The themes related to it can especially shape their lives.

The newest planet, Eris, will hover at barely 23 degrees of Aries from spring 2018 into spring 2019, in conjunction with Baten Kaitos. This provides an intriguing opportunity to observe how the qualities connected to both the planet and the fixed star combine to reflect events in ourselves and the world situation as a whole. A Mars transit in Aries will conjoin Baten Kaitos January 30–February 5, 2019. This is another cycle which can coincide with events connected to this star. Some following the Old Ways might find dedicating an Imbolc ritual to this planetary transit helpful. Use a topaz-colored candle on the altar, perhaps adding a figurine of a sea creature.

—DIKKI-JO MULLEN

Owning the Truth

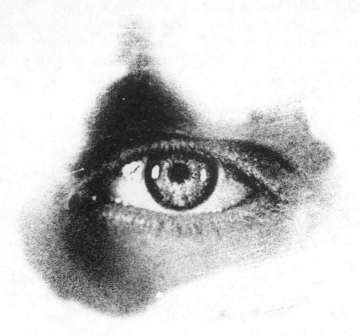

Many in the Pagan and Wiccan community have suffered exclusion from blood family resulting from the choice of the spiritual path we walk. It is rare that rifts can be overcome and true healing can take place. Nick Murphy below shares his moving experience at the deathbed of his most cherished grandmother.

Owning the truth of my Paganism came with a price. I lost the acceptance of family, respect for my mother and the unwavering faith of my grandmother. Only the last loss hurt. When she told me her heart was broken, and laid the superstition and lies of the Christian world at the altar of my Gods I was struck clean through. The passing years and miles left the wound scarred, resentment turning me indifferent and callous. I held back the bottle of my love, pouring sparingly, so as not to waste on thirsty, ungiving ground. Mostly though, I just missed my grandmother. I felt cut adrift, in sight of the shore, welcome to visit and ever judged. The staccato attacks of her ignorance blended with the litany of love so that I was never certain when to flinch. I had lost access to her through the door that to her mattered most, and with it a part of my childhood.

But now she's dying. At 88 an unrelenting drug regimen, dialysis and all the king's men can't put her back together again. Her heart is going, chased closely by her kidneys. Soon the poems and the stories will be gone forever and it turns out it's actually my heart that's broken. And last night, crowded into a hospital room with my wife and the children who adopted me, it all came crashing home. That hurt was about to become forever and all I could think about was praying with my grandmother. I wanted to hold her hands, let pour forth the words and know her again in the halls where lay the strongest part of her heart.

I asked for the room. When only she remained I took her skeletal hands in mine and said "I love you." I kissed her forehead as she had often done mine. She smiled weakly and told me to pray for her. Told me she knew I didn't pray, that I didn't have faith, that I didn't believe. I told her yet again that I do pray, do have faith, do believe. I asked if she would pray with me and agreeing she offered to lead. I asked her to follow and waited for her panic—there was none.

She nodded, we both closed our eyes and my grandmother heard me for the first time in years. I prayed as we pray—calling on our Gods, seeing the line of our people stretch back through our ancestors and forward through the eyes of our children. I gave thanks for this turn on the wheel and spoke of the joy in found again family. I held sacred the Earth, trees, rocks and creatures of all creation, and honored the Lady of the Moon and the Wild God. All that with my eyes closed, my truth battling the fear of what I would see when I opened them again. I blinked through the tears, ready for the dismissal and there, before my very eyes, was my grandmother. She was glowing, bright and strong, and she cupped my face in her hands. She said that she loved my words—now our words—and that she felt God's presence. She told me she heard God in my voice. She made me feel whole again. She made me feel home again.

So I honor the Gods and all of you, and give thanks for all that came from the price I paid. My coven, my family, my wife and the one surprise I never saw coming—my grandmother.

–NICK MURPHY

2018 SUNRISE AND SUNSET TIMES
Providence—San Francisco—Sydney—London

	Sunrise				Sunset			
	Prov	SF	Syd	Lon	Prov	SF	Syd	Lon
Jan 5	7:13	7:26	5:50	8:05	16:29	17:05	20:09	16:07
15	7:11	7:24	5:59	8:00	16:40	17:15	20:08	16:21
25	7:04	7:19	6:09	7:49	16:52	17:26	20:05	16:37
Feb 5	6:54	7:10	6:20	7:32	17:06	17:38	19:57	16:57
15	6:41	6:59	6:29	7:15	17:19	17:49	19:47	17:15
25	6:27	6:47	6:39	6:54	17:31	18:00	19:36	17:34
Mar 5	6:14	6:35	6:45	6:37	17:41	18:07	19:26	17:48
15	5:58	6:21	6:54	6:15	17:52	18:17	19:13	18:05
25	5:41	6:06	7:01	5:52	18:03	18:26	19:00	18:22
Apr 5	5:22	5:49	6:06	5:27	18:16	18:36	17:45	18:40
15	5:06	5:35	6:17	5:05	18:27	18:46	17:32	18:57
25	4:50	5:21	6:24	4:44	18:38	18:55	17:21	19:14
May 5	4:37	5:09	6:32	4:25	18:49	19:04	17:10	19:30
15	4:26	5:00	6:39	4:09	18:59	19:13	17:02	19:46
25	4:17	4:53	6:42	3:56	19:08	19:21	16:56	20:00
June 5	4:12	4:48	6:53	3:46	19:17	19:29	16:53	20:12
15	4:10	4:47	6:58	3:43	19:22	19:33	16:52	20:20
25	4:12	4:49	7:00	3:44	19:25	19:36	16:54	20:22
July 5	4:17	4:54	6:58	3:51	19:24	19:35	16:58	20:19
15	4:24	5:00	6:58	4:01	19:19	19:31	17:04	20:11
25	4:33	5:08	6:53	4:14	19:11	19:24	17:10	20:00
Aug 5	4:44	5:17	6:44	4:30	18:59	19:14	17:18	19:42
15	4:54	5:25	6:34	4:46	18:46	19:02	17:25	19:23
25	5:04	5:34	6:23	5:02	18:30	18:49	17:32	19:02
Sept 5	5:16	5:43	6:08	5:19	18:12	18:33	17:39	18:38
15	5:26	5:52	5:55	5:35	17:55	18:17	17:46	18:15
25	5:36	6:00	5:41	5:51	17:38	18:02	17:53	17:52
Oct 5	5:47	6:09	6:27	6:07	17:21	17:47	18:00	17:29
15	5:58	6:18	6:14	6:24	17:04	17:32	19:08	17:07
25	6:10	6:28	6:02	6:41	16:49	17:19	19:16	16:47
Nov 5	6:23	6:39	5:51	7:01	16:35	17:07	19:26	16:27
15	6:35	6:50	5:43	7:18	16:25	16:58	19:35	16:11
25	6:47	7:01	5:38	7:35	16:18	16:53	19:45	16:00
Dec 5	6:58	7:10	5:37	7:49	16:15	16:51	19:54	15:53
15	7:06	7:18	5:38	8:00	16:16	16:52	20:01	15:52
25	7:12	7:23	5:42	8:05	16:20	16:57	20:07	15:56

Prov=Providence; SF=San Francisco; Syd=Sydney; Lon=London
Times are presented in the standard time of the geographical location, using the current time zone of that place.

Window on the Weather

Since the dawn of time, humankind has pursued the knowledge of things to come with vehemence only matched by the species' will to survive and perpetuate in its time on this green Earth. The pursuit to know the right time to conceive, marry, conquer, travel and sow has been over-riding. Some of the methods employed in these very important pursuits have been esoteric, as well as scientific. Our need to discern future weather conditions has not been exempt from our need to know.

The prediction of weather has moved from the domain of the priest-seer to the domain of the meteorological scientist relying on the review of past data and multiple variables in the present in order to glimpse conditions of the future. While looking into the weather for tomorrow or next week can be a laborious task, forecasting a year can be wrought with intricacies that are complex beyond the imagination.

Meteorologists use many tools to tackle long-term weather forecast-ing. In creating this *Window on the Weather*, our meteorologist Tom Lang, considers orientation of the Earth in its orbit, the irregular shape of orbit, cosmic disturbances such as Sun spots, interstellar radiation and human activity, along with a myriad of other variables that will influence trends for 2018.

SPRING

MARCH 2018. The strongest correlation between variant natural systems and weather patterns include a combination of so called "ENSO" states and solar cycles. The current combination favors lingering winter snow, with the heaviest season snowfalls extending from the southern Appalachians to the Mid-Atlantic States. A second area of heavy snowfall can occur in the southern Rockies. New England and the Ohio Valley will experience below average late winter cold with drier conditions. The coldest air relative to normal occurs across the Great Lakes and Northern Plains while the West Coast experiences generally mild and dry conditions. Southern California receives some wet weather during the first days of Spring.

APRIL 2018. Advancing cold air increases the likelihood for more numerous tornado outbreaks. This is especially true in the United States where over half of all planetary tornadoes occur annually. Especially prone in April are Texas, Oklahoma, as well as the Mississippi and Ohio Valleys, where the greatest clash between warm Gulf of Mexico air and persistent winter cold occurs. Expect at least two such outbreaks this month. This is also blizzard season from the western Plains to the Dakotas and Minnesota. The biggest snowstorm can occur in Denver this month as a Pacific storm arrives without warning. Farther east, a sudden turn to mild weather enhances what would normally be an orderly snow melt with flooding likely from Pennsylvania to New England. While the fire danger remains high in Florida, some tropical moisture brings relief by mid-month and in anticipation of more abundant summer rain. Ground moisture in Kansas and Oklahoma is adequate for Spring planting.

MAY 2018. With a diminished number of sunspots generally, the growing season will only be affected slightly "on the margins." Less solar output means less moisture will be necessary for crops across the Northern Plains. The severe weather season shifts north with more tornadoes reported across central Great Lakes and Ohio Valley. After a severe winter, the weather inverts suddenly with warmer than normal conditions from Florida to Maine. A weak tropical disturbance will bring welcome rain to Florida. Advancing north, wind-driven rain soaks the Carolinas, an unusual weather event for May. The West Coast resumes a warm and dry weather pattern after abundant Winter rainfall. Still, the snowpack remains deep in the Sierra Nevada.

SUMMER

JUNE 2018. Beautiful June weather covers much of the nation with a fine growing season fully underway. The first encounter with high humidity is felt from the Ohio Valley to the Gulf Coast as Gulf of Mexico water temperatures remain above normal. Cool weather lingers across the high plains keeping ground moisture adequate for crops. There is a battle between air masses farther south and east, with rounds of severe weather including an occasional tornado from the mid-Mississippi Valley northeast into New England. Farther south, west winds bring persistent warmth from New York City to Charlotte. While daytime temperatures are hot, relatively low humidity will still bring comfortable night temperatures to that region. Beautiful June weather is felt across the Rockies and Pacific Northwest.

JULY 2018. Midsummer heat is focused in the East this year. Above-normal temperatures can be expected from the Great Lakes to New England and as far south as the Mid-Atlantic. Outdoor enthusiasts should remain alert for late afternoon and evening thunderstorms, a few being severe. Such activity is strongest in hilly terrain, west of the immediate coast. There, cooling sea breezes bring relief from the summer heat and quell such storms to some extent. Vivid thunderstorms are also likely each afternoon along the Continental Divide in the West. These storms are slower moving and locally focused. Vacation travelers should remain alert for flash flooding in river basins. Pleasant breezes are felt along the Pacific Coast.

AUGUST 2018. First stirrings of the hurricane season bring the greatest risk of an August surprise to the Gulf Coast and Atlantic Florida shoreline. Water temperatures remain high there and tropical storms are a normal consequence of that. Hurricanes tend to cluster in frequency during such conditions and can form near land. Residents there and elsewhere along the Eastern Seaboard should remain watchful during the entire hurricane season which lasts through the end of November. Two monsoonal flows bring abundant rainfall to the U.S. One exists from the Gulf Coast and extends along the Appalachians and into New England. The other persists from northern Arizona northward to Wyoming. Most rainfall there occurs in mountainous terrain. Afternoon and evening thunder is also heard across the Northern Plains and Great Lake states.

AUTUMN

SEPTEMBER 2018. The peak of the hurricane seasons sparks keen interest along the U.S. coast. Storms can occur suddenly in the Bahamas and elsewhere throughout the near Atlantic. The risk of a sudden move from such a storm northward to New England is present this year. Elsewhere, the weather is relatively tranquil across the nation's heartland. Notably, an early frost occurs in western Montana and northern Idaho by the 20th and the Tetons are dusted by snow. This occurs as fire danger increases in Washington and Oregon on the windward side of the Cascades. Dry conditions spread south through California and monsoonal rains ease across the Great Basin as southeast winds increase throughout the "Four Corners." Fire danger is also high in southeast Utah and Colorado.

OCTOBER 2018. On average, October brings the most stable weather to the Northern Hemisphere as the days shorten and temperatures cool. Notable hibernating behavior is exhibited by all mammals this year.

During the past four years, it is notable that mid and high latitude fertility rates have slowed considerably. This is part of natural variance and a pattern that will persist until the next solar minimum. This pattern is also consistent with slowing mammalian activity in general during the fall, as winter approaches and the first frosts are felt in Northern Valleys. As shadows lengthen farther south, dry weather persists with rains confined to the Gulf Coast and Florida. Fall foliage is especially brilliant this year with plentiful summer rainfall.

NOVEMBER 2018. Fall weather turns crisp this month, though precipitation remains sparse in many places. The West is particularly dry as high pressure dominates the region and southeast air brings Santa Anna winds to southern California. Fires are a concern along coastal ranges with the driest air late each afternoon. The last of the fall harvest is accompanied by dry weather in the Southern Plains, while the first dusting of snow coats the Northern Plains with heavier snows in the Rockies. A tropical storm near Bermuda approaches and combines with another cyclone to bring windswept rains and gales to the Northeast. This ends the foliage season abruptly throughout the Mid-Atlantic. A brief lake effect snowfall snarls travel in western New York State and northeast Ohio around Thanksgiving.

WINTER

DECEMBER 2018. Winter begins with its first month bringing cold weather in stages. Generally, the coldest weather lasts two or three days and this year is focused from the Great Lakes through the Ohio Valley and Northeast through the Mid-Atlantic. The Southeast, Arizona and Southern California experience above normal temperatures. Though generally dry for now, arctic air encountering the unfrozen Great lakes provide western New York State, Pennsylvania and Michigan lake effect snow which can hamper travel. Lighter snows fall as far south as the Mason Dixon and are slow to melt, given the low sun angle and advancing cold. An ice storm is a risk this year from the Ohio Valley to New England after the 20th. Dry weather persists along the West Coast.

JANUARY 2019. Some of the coldest winters on record have occurred during similar times as these, when low solar output is combined with a La Niña ENSO state. This correlates well with arctic air, originating in Siberia, that crosses the North Pole and advances to cover much of the continent east of the Rockies. Occasional ocean storms develop with high risk of heavy snowfall for all cities along the East Coast. This happens several times followed by brutally cold air, especially across the Great Lakes and New England. West of the Rockies the weather is unseasonably mild and dry along much of the West Coast. Rain is confined to coastal Oregon and Washington State.

February 2019. The coldest air of the year is felt throughout the entire east until the tenth, when the Sun's advance takes hold and eases the worst of the cold. Still, energy is provided for more intense storms with heavy snow falling again from New England through the Ohio Valley. Colder water temperatures tend to "capture" storms and slows their advance away from the coast. A storm or two lasting two or three days is possible under these conditions. Snow is also likely from Denver to Dallas this month as winter arrives late there. Winter wheat may be affected in Kansas while a more persistent snow cover will likely protect crops farther north. Pacific storms finally advance on the West Coast, alleviating dry conditions there. Several gale centers will sweep the immediate coast with high winds from Central California northward.

SEER STONES

ONE OF THE MOST well-known devices for predicting the future is the crystal ball, but it's not the only method of scrying. Seer stones, also called peep stones, were once a popular way of discovering the secrets of the unknown.

Unlike the crystal ball or the black mirror, the seer stone doesn't have to be reflective or translucent. The legendary Brahan Seer of 17th century Scotland allegedly used an adder stone.

Serpent's Kiss
Called adder stones because the Druids believed they were formed from the hardened saliva of the common European adder (Vipera berus). Adder stones have natural holes in the middle through which the Seer looks to glimpse visions, though Druids didn't originate this practice. Pliny the Elder referred to them as an existing phenomenon in his Natural History, which he completed before his death in AD 79.

In book XXII, he describes how the stones are created:

"A vast number of serpents are twisted together in summer, and coiled up in an artificial knot by their saliva and slime; and this is called 'the serpent's egg'. The druids say that it is tossed in the air with hissings and must be caught in a cloak before it touches the earth."

Pliny doesn't mention their use in divination but instead acknowledges their use for "gaining lawsuits, and access to kings."

Fairy Glimpses
More English Fairy Tales by Joseph Jacobs (1894) alludes to the belief that looking through a "self-bored stone" allows one to see the fairies. Unlike the holes found in stones on a seashore, the hole in a self-bored stone is made by running freshwater. In "Habetrot and

Scantlie Mab," a tale included in this collection, not only can mortals see the fairies through them, but see their true selves.

Divine Visions

Lithomancy, the form of divination using stones, includes not only the holed and reflective variety but also solid, dull stones.

From the age of Justinian comes a tale of a physician named Eusebius who carried an oracular stone called a baetulum. It was spherical, white and approximately the width of a person's palm. When one posed a question to the stone, characters appeared upon the surface and it emitted sounds like those of a shrill pipe.

Joseph Smith, the founder of the Church of Jesus Christ of Latter Day Saints, employed a similar type of seer stone as an aid in translating the *Book of Mormon* from golden plates that the angel Moroni revealed to him. His was neither reflective nor holed, but was a whitish stone about the size of a hen's egg. Instead of being a solid color the stone had layers of different hues.

Smith took the stone and dropped it into his hat, then put his face into the top of the hat, pulling the edges close to exclude light. Using this common method of scrying with a seer stone he reported he could see something.

Later he repeated the operation. What appeared to be a piece of parchment materialized on the stone. On top of that, a single character and an interpretation of that character in English emerged. Smith would dictate the English translation to his scribe, Oliver Cowdery. Cowdery read it back and when Smith indicated the transcription was correct, the character would disappear and a new one replace it.

Eventually Smith would not use the stones at all, relying instead on direct divine revelation.

—MORVEN WESTFIELD

Leave Your Bundle at the Hedge
A meditation in seeing with Other eyes

WHAT WOULD IT mean to bundle up your assumptions and your cherished opinions about the world, your membership to interest groups and ways of life, your nationality and identifiers—the things the world tells you make you *you*—and leave them in a bundle at the hedge? Quite simply, to us as to our forebears, this means something like death. Only the dead get to see with eyes clear of allegiance. Initiation into Witchcraft, not the ritual that confirms it for your community necessarily, but the thing itself, should give you a glimpse through those eyes. If it doesn't then something isn't working to its full potential.

Liminality

Imagine that your town or city bordered a wild forest region. Moving through that edge place is a people utterly alien to the way of life you've grown up with. I don't mean pleasantly quirky or fashionably 'fringe,' I mean shocking and discomfortingly Other. You might like to imagine them as denizens of Faerie, Witches or travelling folk of some unknown stripe.

In this liminal space, the edge of the wild, you have met with one of their people and struck up a unique bond. Something inside you has quickened in their presence, something beyond explanation, even whilst they make you uncomfortable at times. The old primal voices of the body are making decisions for you. Your guts and bones decide to escape into an unknown future while your brain is still floundering for equilibrium. Their caravan leaves at

dawn. Before you jump the hedge and enter the forest they have asked you to leave all your belongings in a bundle by the hedge, as a symbol of your commitment to Leaving.

When the Otherworld touches you, things are not always as they seem. This is no ordinary bundle and these are no ordinary possessions you've been asked to leave behind, just as the hedge we cross is no ordinary hedge. The things you place inside the bundle are preconceptions, ideologies and affiliations from within the world of man—identity markers that may even be painfully important to you. They are the things you have believed all your life make you different, special, uniquely flawed, uniquely wonderful. They are the water the fish can't see because it has swum all its life in it. These are the things that must be sacrificed to truly, deeply, cross the hedge and find the astral Witches' Sabbat. This eternal Sabbat is always happening at the true midnight of the soul but is obscured from daylight eyes by a film of forgetfulness.

It is arguable (like finding the darkness and stillness I discussed in my last article *The Night-Time Mind of the Witch* for *The Witches' Almanac Spring 2014 to Spring 2015 Issue 33*) that it's becoming harder and harder for us moderns to locate what 'possessions' need to go into the bundle and be left behind. The world of man has become so immersive. The reign of ideology cushions us from the full sensual experience of reality and obscures the many options still open to us.

Do we know whether these Others we are about to leave with will care about or subscribe in any way to anything resembling our politics? Our opinions? Why are we leaving with them when the crooked path their caravan will take through the woods is so unpredictable? All we know about them is that these strangers *personify* Witchcraft—the true, deep-veined current in all its unsettling and *unheimlich* glory, pulsing with the dark light of Luciferic revelation.

Unseen Dangers

The risk inherent in this story of mad commitment mirrors the fact that no matter how you come to Witchcraft there is no way to fully know what's inside its Pandora's box until one opens it. Commitments are made before full knowledge becomes possible, not the other way around. The fruit on the Tree of Knowledge is bitten into before it's experienced and there is no uneating it.

Yet coming with questions is a good sign. As you stand before the hedge, ready to make your assay into the heart of Witchcraft and the eternal Sabbat, your questions are both necessary and futile. No matter how long you've been walking the path you are always in this same position every day, deciding whether you want to go deeper into the forest or stop where you are.

When you truly comprehend the depths of alienation necessary to abandon the bundle you will see why there is only one good reason to make this crossing: because you have no choice. Unless you know in yourself the alien and find a wild trust because you trust in yourself, unless you know in yourself the foreigner, the misfit, the Other, the scapegoat, (not in a romanticized way, but as an inescapable reality you are willing to pass through discomfort to understand) then there is no place for you out there. You should stay within the walled places, the fenced yards and the hedged gardens. In truth there is no shame in knowing what you're ready for and what you're not.

The backwards-tending dances and images of ritual inversion are only a code for this ultimate act of dissociation from the thinking of mankind you must accomplish. Witchcraft does not so much turn established order on its head by opposing it in a reactionary manner, it throws the whole board up in the air. So to really know what should go into your bundle you are going to need a practice that brings on a dissociative state. In place of shortcuts via entheogens and the more extreme measures such as fasting and dance until collapse, the best clues are found in behavior the world rejects.

In a world permeated by electric light, sitting alone in the dark has become a sign for concern, walking out alone in the dark a cause for fear. Sitting alone in the dark on the edge of a wild place and gazing back upon the world a time-wasting form of productivity sacrilege. But this is exactly what you must do, if your state or country controls the plant and fungal helpers that once ushered us into the right state to perceive ourselves as an outside intelligence might perceive us. This is what you must do to properly fill the bundle of your old ideas and habits.

Otherwise you will not be able to see them because they are still what you use to *see with*. You must complete a pilgrimage to such a place where you can look back at the world of man as though from outside it. Imagine you do not come from there, that you know

88

nothing of its ways, forget your birth language, forget any human language. Imagine you have come out of the trees behind you and are regarding with little knowledge this world so lit up that it obscures the stars...

How would you see if you were without the most basic assumptions of that world out there? It might help to begin by thinking about what those assumptions are precisely. From the lights that burn all through the night you can tell one immediate ruling assumption, light is safer than darkness. People you haven't met yet blazon this belief to the heavens. What else do they believe? What do they take as a given? If the idea of being without those givens doesn't disturb you at least a little then you haven't really thought about it enough yet.

Necessary Disorientation

If this exercise makes you feel comfortable, if you can reassure yourself that you've already done all this and don't need to again, that you've already removed the blinkers put upon you by society, this is an immediate sign you need to do it again. Stepping Out isn't just about going to higher ground or a place outside the town and casting your eyes back in, leaving your previous ways of thinking in a bundle at the hedge, it is about seeing with the eyes of one alien to this world.

Through an act of will and imagination one must slough off everything—nationality, gender, your mother-tongue, your species—until you are down to your bare bones with reality. Only when you get down to the last ways in which the world can still manipulate your thinking, accept the assumptions you barely even realize you carry from childhood, are you empowered to truly step back inside that system and not just bring but *be* change.

You need to imagine while you're preparing to do it, conjuring the glamour of this phantasy with all your cunning fire, that everything you own is in the bundle. All your possessions, your ID cards, the title deeds to any properties you own, your childhood keepsakes, even letters from your dead grandparents, everything.

On the other side of that hedge or gate you must pass is a whole other style of life you can't even fully imagine. It's an important part of the glamour you are creating that you acknowledge your lack of knowledge. Because outside that hedge, the life you must see as waiting for you contains your own wild self. It contains a life run by the principles of animism and your humility is your first gift to it. Just as your first gift to an indigenous people whose culture you have no way of understanding is to admit your ignorance and place down as an offering your willingness to learn. This won't include impressing them by telling them all your own wonderful observations and opinions about magic so you can share your perspective with them. It will include your quietude. Only an empty cup can be filled.

Imagine that when you step through the Hedge this other life will literally have you. There won't be warm beds and security where you're going. You

must see it as literal or the magic of it won't fully work. You must imagine you will be living off your wits and the bonds you form with those around you. Until you've decided firstly that you would be willing, if you had the option to leave your modern Western life behind, to pursue the Craft and re-find your wild self, then you have no business with Witchcraft. This is not a path of safety or security.

Bare Before the Spirits

When you have constructed this phantasy so strongly that you all but expect horses to erupt from the trees with elfish people of the woods riding them, you are ready to place your bundle. If the glamour your thoughts create is strong enough it won't matter what's really in the bundle. Only that you sit with the feeling of leaving behind all those markers of your ego—not only the objects, but the cherished belief patterns and long-held opinions. Choose for this magic a place where you will be able to have privacy. If you don't feel assured of this, it is a sign you haven't gone far enough into the wild.

Where it is possible your human clothes can be stuffed into the bundle at the hedge and you go on naked. Just like some tales of the Witch Goddess both in Wicca and the tale of Inanna you are being stripped of the markers of selfhood as you descend to the Underworld. Here you must wash. Ideally it would be in a Moon-drenched pool, deep, dark and bone-achingly cold enough to simulate your descent into the womb of making and un-being we call the Underworld.

If this is entirely impossible take with you water from spring or wave in which you can wash beneath the Moon. As you do so consciously cleanse yourself of your baptism into any faith or ideology you have previously been. No value judgment of these creeds or factions is necessary. The helpful will be washed away with the unhelpful. Capitalism is as much a religion as Catholicism. All isms must be washed away.

When this is done you will clean your nails in the most scrupulous way you've ever done before, both with water and an implement. Remember the Witches of old who cleaned their nails and asked God and the ways of Christ to be as far from them as dirt was from their nails. After it is done you will declare (your first words spoken aloud since passing the hedge): 'May my soul be as clear of all creeds and systems as my nails are free from dirt.' Then you will symbolically sharpen them.

When this is done allow the water to dry on your body. Allow the feeling of emptiness to call to the Unseen like a vacuum of force waiting to be filled. For there is no such thing as a position to stand outside of other things, only a temporary glamour that allows us to see the truth of our predicament. Looking back with the eyes of one who has shed their skin, the world on the other side of the hedge may look very different to you. But just by having taken this advice, just by creating the poetry in your mind of inside and outside, us

and them, you have already sided with something. The temporary vacuum state of shedding calls for renewal, for fertilization. Without explicitly needing to say so, just by Stepping Out you have already taken on the perspective of the Otherwise and aligned yourself with the internal myth of Witchcraft.

Here, if you have not done so already in your Tradition or practice, you can call out to the Unseen and affirm this allegiance with the Other, or simply repeat it if you have already taken oaths. However you choose to do so make it wild and real. Make it come up from the depths of yourself or don't bother calling at all.

You might do this by shouting three times: 'Robin Goodfellow!' or freed as you now are from religious fears and stigmas, you could call him devil, angel, faerie, incubus, god, monster—whatever words stir fear and desire in you. Take the posture of one hand above your head the other under your foot. If you have truly stripped yourself bare of all other attachments and left your old self at the hedge, for the first time you will understand what this gesture really means.

As you have had a chance to return to your home and ordinary life, not been carried away by a faerie people to live in the forest, it is highly likely that many repeats of leaving the bundle could be required over time. Whenever we feel that our personal power is getting swept away by the affairs of the world and we are being pulled along rather than being the world-movers and world-shakers we were meant to be, it can pay to repeat this working.

–LEE MORGAN

The Magick of Mortar & Pestle

Witches have long been associated with magical plants, potions and brews. One of the old arts of Witchcraft is the use of herbs. The primary tool of this Old World Witchery is the mortar and pestle set—essential tool when working with Green Wood Magic. In mystical terms the mortar represents the womb gate, the source through which things manifest in the material world. By extension it can be thought of as the earth envisioned as a cauldron that generates life and draws it back into itself again. For those who seek a religious or spiritual connotation, the mortar can represent the Womb of the Great Mother Goddess.

As a ritual and magical tool the mortar (in some traditions of Witchcraft) is called Life-giver as well as Death-taker. It connects with the former nature through which it can be used to generate and to reanimate. For the latter it's used to terminate and to decompose. As a tool, the mortar can be made of wood or mineral. Wood mortars are ideal for working with plant spirits and mineral ones are good for working with the organic memory of the earth (the terrestrial counterpart of the Akashic Records).

To prepare your mortar, perform the following:

Place the mortar out beneath the Full Moon when it's high overhead in the night sky. Encircle it with white rose petals. Use candles for lighting during this preparation. Pour fresh water into the mortar (about two thirds filled) and then pick it up in both hands. Hold the mortar so the Moon above you is reflected on the water. Speak these words:

Queen of light in the night sky bright,
I call you to this Witch's rite.
Enter this mortar, imbue this womb,
Enter this mortar, imbue this tomb

Continue holding the mortar up and turn yourself in a full circle, clockwise, saying:

Life-giver, womb-birther,
*   mother of all,*
Open to the lighted world,
*   come to the call*

Next, turn in a full circle, counterclockwise, saying:

Death-taker, tomb-maker,
*   receiver of all,*
Open to the world of black,
*   come to the call*

Pour the water out of the mortar directly into the earth. Next set the mortar on the ground and replenish the water. After this, pick up the pestle in your left hand positioning yourself so you see the Moon on the surface of the water in the mortar. Then dip the pestle into the water and stir it slowly in a clockwise manner while you say:

Queen of light in the night sky bright,
I call you to this Witch's rite.
Enter this pestle, deep inside,
Grant me the power to stir the tide

Now hold up the pestle up to the Moon and turn yourself clockwise in a full circle saying:

Horn awakener, seed-bearer,
generator of all,
Rise to the lighted world, come
to the call

Next, turn counterclockwise in a full circle saying:

Serpent slumberer, life-gatherer,
witherer of all,
Open to the world of black,
come to the call

Set the mortar and pestle down separately side by side. Look at the Moon with your left eye (right eye closed) and place your palm (left hand) beneath the Moon as though cupping it.

Place the palm of your right hand over the mortar and say:

Mortar of the Witches' Craft, by art
of magic in the night,
To you I pass the blessed Moons
bright and sacred light

Next, place the palm of your right hand over the pestle and say:

Pestle of the Witches' Craft, by art of
magic in the night,
To you I pass the blessed Moons
bright and sacred light

Set the pestle inside the mortar, place both palms over the set and say:

Womb at the center of all things,
Shaper, transformer, and birther of all,
Hold or free spirits that come
to the call,
Life-giver, Death-taker,
Stone carver, dream maker,
I turn the Wheel, then to show,
And what I spin, it now is so

Clap your hands three times and place both palms back over the mortar & pestle, saying:

Tree at the center of all things,
Tower from where enchantment sings,
Thresher, dream-churner, joiner of all,
Sound for the spirits to come at
my call

Complete by drying the mortar and pestle and taking them away in a wrapped cloth. Leave them wrapped until the next night.

The basic magical use of the mortar and pestle is for "calling in" and "sending off." The former involves stirring the mortar with the pestle in a clockwise motion (also know as deosil). To release or send away uses the opposite direction (counterclockwise or widdershins).

Before beginning with any spell work, first enchant the tools. To do this, place the pestle in the mortar and begin tapping back and forth against the inner sides of the mortar. Do this in a slow, deliberate and even tempo. Next you will draw upon the creative cycle of the Greenwood Realm by aligning with its grow cycle. Simply keep tapping and say these words in keeping with the rhythm:

Seed to crown,
Crown to stem,
Stem to leaf
Leaf to bud,
Bud to flower,
Flower to fruit,
Fruit to seed

Repeat this three times.

The next motion is "circling" the pestle inside the mortar against its inner wall. To perform the intended spell, begin by placing the mortar on its side. Insert the pestle, rotating it clockwise against the inside edge of the mortar. Begin moving slowly and then speed up the motion. Say the incantation and then pause to state your desire. Repeat the incantation for a total of three rounds.

Turn the Wheel
Set the task
Bring to me
The thing I ask
[state intent]

Once the incantations have been completed, hold the mortar in one hand and the pestle in the other. Present them to each cardinal point (east, south, west, north) and say:

By all Forces and Powers that aid the
*   Witches' will*
Go now to the four winds; return my
*   desire fulfilled.*

For sending something away, begin with the same technique of placing the mortar on its side. The pestle then is inserted inside the mortar and rotated counter-clockwise against the edge of the mortar. Use the same motion slowly building up speed with the pestle. Say the incantation and pause to state your desire, repeating the full incantation for a total of three rounds.

Turn the Wheel
Break the cask
Send away
The thing I ask
[state intent]

Once the incantations have been completed, hold the mortar in one hand and the pestle in the other. Present them to each cardinal point (east, south, west, north) and say:

All Force and Powers of the Ways,
*   each measured in store*
Carry my desire off to the four
*   winds, to return no more."*

—RAVEN GRIMASSI

EWÉ

Herbs, Divination and Medicine in Ifá

THE YORUBA of Southwestern Nigeria have a long and rich history of using plants for spiritual and corporal medicines. While many modern ethnic Yorubas will seek rcsolution to their pressing problems by very modern means, they will still bolster their chances with the advice and remedies found in indigenous faiths and attendant pantheon of deities (Òrìṣà). The spiritual heritage of the Òrìṣà preserve a rich body of knowledge of the use of plants and incantations. The lore associated with each individual herb and proper use is embedded in songs, myths and the poetic corpus preserved in the divination systems of Ifá and individual Òrìṣà.

While the priests of each Òrìṣà are schooled in the fundamentals (such as creating lustral waters and initiations), for the most part the diviners in each become the master herbalists. Divination is an oral tradition—lore being committed to writing only arrived recently—passed on through generations from teacher to future diviner. Further, it is the priest-diviners of Ifá—babaláwo (males) or ìyánífá (females)—who are charged with preserving an all-inclusive corpus, inasmuch as within the poetic corpus of Ifá are the verses of the individual Òrìṣà's divination poetry.

Ifá is an extensive divination system composed of 256 oracular signs (Odù Ifá). Each of these signs has a variety of prescribed medicines (spiritual remedies) and sacrifices necessary to easing the life of the religious adherent. To the outsider, the system of Ifá presents as a simple method divination. There are 16 primary signs, which are paired to produce a twofold sign. The first 16 of the Odù Ifá are made of a pairing of the sixteen primaries creating 16 doubles, and 240 secondary signs that result from the pairing of non-matching primaries. The pairing is said to have two legs, each leg being a single primary. The priest of Ifá will generate one of these 256 Odù Ifá by means of manipulation of the tools they received during their initiation. (See http://thewitchesalmanac.com/AlmanacExtras/yoruba.html for a more complete explanation on Ifá.)

Each of the Odù Ifá is accompanied by many poems (Èsè Ifá) that are recited to the client to illuminate the meaning behind the Odù Ifá that has been generated. These poems—taught to and memorized by the apprentice (ọ̀mọ̀ áwo)—are the source of remedies to be prescribed by the babaláwo. Although the ordinary lay person might not understand the cryptic meaning of the Èsè Ifá (except it being explained by the diviner), buried within each poem there is remedial clues. The babaláwo will ascertain the ingredients for ẹbọ (sacrifice) that must be made to ward off evil or assure success. The verses chosen by the babaláwo also contain an indication of the plants to be used to make medicines and the chants (ọfọ̀ àṣẹ) that must be recited in order to activate the efficacy of the ingredients.

The babaláwo will choose the Èsè Ifá that is a verbal link between the problem at hand—the necessary magical action and the Odù Ifá. By means of interrogatory and àṣẹ, the babaláwo will discern the problem and resolution, cleverly navigating the linguistic puns present in the chosen Èsè Ifá. It is these layers (manipulation of divination tools, Èsè Ifá and associated medicines) and verbal gymnastics that are committed to memory. While the modern student will often commit the Èsè Ifá to writing for ease of study, the magico-medicinal properties are only affected by means of verbal recitation. Without verbalization, the incantation (ọfọ̀ àṣẹ) lacks power/energy (àṣẹ). It is rhythm and breath as taught by the babaláwo to the ọ̀mọ̀ áwo which is important. Knowledge of the incantation is essential, as it contains the "power-to-alter."

The types of plants and medicines that can be found in the Èsè Ifá for the most part fit into generalized categories:

Òrìṣà—formulae for "magical works" relating to worshiping of Yoruba deities

Àwúre—beneficent works

Àbìlù—evil works

Ìdáàbòbò—protective works

While this may be a convenient method of categorizing various medicines, some will by nature fall into more than one category. For instance, an Èsè Ifá and indicated ingredients that can be used to cure someone of dysentery, may also be used to give an enemy a case of severe diarrhea. It is difficult to separate plants that belong in the magical category from those that belong in the healing category as they are both intertwined.

It is the constituent parts of the Èsè Ifá that present the diviner with the necessary information that the babaláwo will use. For the most part, each poem contains the following:

1. The alias of the particular Odù Ifá chanted during the present day divination

2. The name of the diviner performing the consultation (this can be one, many diviners)

3. The name of the client (as above, this can be one or more clients)
4. The reason for the divination or the question at hand
5. The advice (sacrifice and possible medicine) provided by the mythological babaláwo
6. Whether the mythological client performed the sacrifice and received medicine

The Odù Ifá is rarely used without changing the name of the second leg, creating an alias. Each Odù Ifá will have many aliases. It is by knowing the problem presented by the client through being informed directly and aṣe that the diviner knows the correct alias to choose and resultant chant.

For example Òsá méjì might be the sign which is presented for the client who needs to curry the favor of Witches. In this case, the babaláwo would say that "Òsá Ẹléyẹ has come to the mat" or "Òsá-the-bird-owner has come to the mat." The-bird-owner is a direct reference to the Witches and is the alias of Òsá méjì. The babaláwo might chant:

Àjẹ́ ń ké kára kára.
Wọ́n ní ẹyẹ òrò ló ọfọ̀ wọ̀lú
Àkàrà oṣó kì í jẹ́ kí ájẹ́ kó pa oṣó
Àjẹ́ kòbàlé ó ní kí ẹyẹ ó má bà lé mi...

Witches shout loud.
They say an evil bird has entered the town.
But the cake of a wizard does not allow them to kill the wizard.
The-witches-do-not-perch-on-me says that the bird will not perch on me...

This opening to this particular Èsè Ifá is the name of a mythological babaláwo who performed the divination and for whom this sign presented. (See Part 2 of the oracular poem referenced above.) It is the name of the diviner (in this case) that is the indication of what the elements of medicine are and the incantation (ọfọ̀ àṣẹ) to be used. The ingredients being fruit of *Cnestis Ferruginea*, Connaraceae and leaf of *Croton Zambesicus*, Euphorbiaceae. These ingredients would be burnt to ash, put on a divining tray and into the ash the babaláwo would to mark the sign of Òsá méjì while he recited the following incantation:

Àjẹ́ ń ké kára kára
Wọ́n ní ẹyẹ òrò ló wọ̀lú
Àkàrà oṣó kì í jẹ́ kí ájẹ́ kó pa oṣó
Àjẹ́ kòbàlé ó ní kí ẹyẹ ó má bà lé mi

The Witches roar
They say malevolent birds have arrived in town
Àkàrà oṣó will never allow the Witch to kill the wizard
Àjẹ́ kòbàlé says the bird should not perch on me

After chanting the incantation the babaláwo would mix the ash with palm oil. He would then give it to the client instructing her or him that from time to time they should put a bit of medicine in their palm and lick it.

Let's look a little closer at this particular Èsè Ifá, alias, incantation and the constituent plants of the medicine. As stated above Ọsá-the-bird-owner is the "chosen" alias. In other words, the babaláwo was moved because of one or several reasons to choose this alias. His first action is to chant the poem. The opening verse contains the medicine encoded in the name of the babaláwo who performed the divination and as well as the result, if the incantation is performed. The first two lines indicates the Witches of the town need to be appeased. Àkàrà oṣó is the fruit *Cnestis Ferruginea*, Connaraceae and Ewé Àjẹ́ kòbàlé is the leaf of *Croton Zambesicus*, Euphorbiaceae. What is not immediately apparent to the non-Yoruba speaker is that there are puns not everyone will catch. To translate them would not do justice. Àkàrà oṣó points to the loudness of the birds (Witches) and Àjẹ́ kòbàlé

indicates not only the blood of witches, but also reverence of the witches.

Not unlike many traditional societies, the Yoruba name of a plant and its qualities have a direct relationship. This has been lost in large part to the everyday person, but remains the providence of the indigenous priests and shamans. The training priest or diviner in Yorubaland will know plants received their names because of their virtues and the play on words not only has its place in the divination but also an activating incantation. In most instances, without speaking the words over the plants they are simply inert waste.

Lastly, there are certain Odù Ifá considered so "hot" that only the most competent babaláwo or ìyánífá would dare to pronounce the poem and incantation. In this case, the names of the plants become the incantation as they are used.

The diviner-priests have many tools at their disposal, not least of which are a sharp tongue, a quick wit and an intelligent plant.

—IFADOYIN SANGOMUYIWA

Eesun awo igbo,

Eruwa awo odan,

Ti tilo le e fawo b'seo

Jigbini bun, o ya a

Oni bawo ni oun le ririe bayi

Won ni ibo ni waru

O si ru,

Igba to rubo tan

Ha bere si iri opolop ire

Observe the creeping plant

How it only thrives in the forest

Whereas the giant-grass does better in the plain.

Thus declared Ifa to Jigbini , the shrub

When it consulted the oracle, asking

"How it might change failure in life into prosperity"

"Offer sacrifice," the oracle replied

Jigbini offered sacrifice and received manifold blessings

Excerpt from Okanran Meji Divination Poem

The Tears of Frankincense

Six Millennia of Sanctity

The precious liquid emerges from the sacred tree when its bark is cut. This sap, the life force of the tree, hardens into small pieces which turn brittle and glitter. Carefully the dried resin is collected about a month after the cutting has occurred. These tiny golden-colored botanical bits and pieces, called the "tears," have been treasured for over 6000 years. Several different trees in the boswellia family will produce the desired resin. When burned, usually on a piece of pure charcoal, a supernatural power emerges. Frankincense is a superb natural incense, deeply symbolic and considered essential to ritual work by many

craft practitioners. Metaphysically, the high frequency of its fragrance creates an aromatherapy which connects directly to opening the crown chakra.

The sacred smoke is credited with soothing and calming a troubled mind, casting away negativity and karma while preparing the atmosphere to set desired intentions. Frankincense has been burned in temples, churches, yoga ashrams and craft circles to honor and invoke the favor of the Gods and Goddesses. Ayurvedic medicine uses it to drive away diseases and encourage improved health. It emits a precious essence as it burns which facilitates healing on many

levels. As an oil or when made into a salve, frankincense has been used to relieve the pain of arthritis.

The name frankincense hints at the role Frankish traders played in introducing it to the West, but it actually derives from an Old English phrase (franc incens) which refers to its quality. Sometimes the tears are diffused into oil for use in anointing or burning instead of the hardened resin or tears.

A few remote regions around the globe provide the right climate to grow the mystical and powerful trees which yield frankincense tears. Places where the trees can be found growing include areas around Oman in Ethiopia, Somalia and the Indian Himalayas. The resin from Somalia has a deep balsamic scent. Frankincense from other regions tends to be lighter and sweeter in aroma. This ancient and traditional incense is always a powerful aid in ritual work. The different varieties are all desirable and the selection of which to use is a matter of personal preference. Frankincense or its close cousin olibanum can be purchased at metaphysical and religious supply stores. In magical workings it is linked to the Sun.

An easy and powerful house blessing can be done using frankincense. This is especially good to do during times when situations just seem difficult. First open the doors and windows for a few minutes early in the day to invite in fresh air and sunlight while encouraging any negative energies or bad luck to disperse. It helps to follow this by thoroughly cleaning the premises. As sunset nears allow a few of the tears of frankincense to smolder on a burning piece of charcoal in a thurible or incense burner. Ring a bell three times then carry the fragrant burning incense around the inside of the premises. Give thanks to the Lord and Lady for inspiration, growth and improved good fortune. Once the charcoal has burned out allow intuition to guide you as to whether to cast any remaining ashes either onto the earth or into the wind.

—GRANIA LING

The Bell
The Symbol Clearly Rings True

THE FAMED MAGICIAN Aleister Crowley listed bells among those essential tools needed for effectively practicing the occult arts. Long cherished as amulets and collectibles, bells represent acknowledging and reaching out to divine forces. They are a voice for starting events in motion.

The sound, which can carry across vast distances, evokes a powerful call—a grab for attention. Summoning, warning, healing, celebrating and mourning are among the rituals which have been associated with bell ringing for thousands of years. These hollow cup-like vessels made of metal, ceramic, shells, wood and other materials will make a sound either when struck by a clapper suspended from within or tapped on the outside with some type of wand or hammer. Bells are found among the remains of the earliest civilizations. The word for these special and enigmatic objects may have originated with a supernatural being named Bel or Ba'al, a Babylonian earth god. As an inhabitant of the earth plane, Bel was of neither Heaven nor Hell, alternating instead between good and evil.

Bell, Book and Candle, a classic movie (1958) about witchcraft references a curse performed using a bell. A famous line from another long-time favorite film *It's a Wonderful Life* (1946) reads "Every time a bell rings an angel gets its wings." The saying predates the movie by at least a century and hints at angelic invocations involving bells. In religious texts the ringing bells accompany the opening of

the gates of Heaven. A bell ringing can also inspire fear and dread, for it has an association with warnings. "Ask not for whom the bell tolls" references the bell as a symbol of mortality. The loud, bright sound fades after being rung, then stops completely. The analogy is that a particular event starts and finishes, as does the span of life.

Ringing bells evoke a conditioned response. Holiday bells usher in the Yuletide spirit. A doorbell signals the arrival of someone desiring entrance while a school bell signals the beginning and end of a study period. Long before text messages were used to contact loved ones dinner bells were rung as a message to hurry home at the end of the day. The association of bells with weddings and other sacraments can

be traced back to the 6th century C.E. The sound was used to both announce celebrations and protect from harm. Inscriptions and prayers or personal names have been inscribed upon bells, presumably to amplify a blessing or message each time it is rung. In Colonial America beloved bell towers have great prominence. Paul Revere, a member of the Freemasons in high standing, has many historical associations with the mystique of bells. This influential patriot cast at least 23 bells over several decades including the ones dedicated for his own Second Church of Boston and the famous sailing vessel, Old Ironsides.

The mysterious phrase "belling the stag" hints at a link between the Pagan god Cerrunnos and bells. The stag's bells suggest a fertility blessing for agriculture. Cowbells have a dual use too, being used to track the movements of the herd while also keeping away evil spirits. The same is true of sleigh bells. Small bells are worn worldwide as amulets to invoke both joy and protection. Jesters wore belled caps to warn of trickery. A folk tale about "belling a cat" also suggests how bells are used to warn of impending threats. Spiritualists will usually ring a bell at the beginning and end of a séance to welcome and later release spirit entities.

The geographical location of bells as well as their sizes and distributions define status and culture. Queen Elizabeth of England's Diamond Jubilee in 2012 was announced by eight gigantic bells cast for the occasion. Siberian shamans rang bells to punctuate incantations. In parts of Asia a fading bell tone is taken as a significant omen. Huge, loud bells in Russian Orthodox practices represent authority and the voice of God. Buddhists use consecrated bells in spiritual practices. Contemporary Western Civilization has a tradition of bells regulating the day through tolling the hours. Bell ringing serves in a wide variety of ways to warn, announce events and rejoice.

The careful selection of the perfect bell as a tool of art by those who would follow the path of the witch can greatly enhance ritual practices and spell casting. Upon choosing one, fill the cup with a strong infusion of rosemary and spring water. Sip the liquid, then ring the bell six times. This will assure a beautiful voice and eloquent command of language.

— KATHRYN MUELLER

104

La Santa Muerte

A SKELETAL WOMAN in a bountiful wedding dress, cloaked in gold, clutches a scythe. A silvery white tiara adorns her pale skull. This is only one representation of the Skeleton Saint. Also known as La Niña Blanca (the White Girl), The Bony Lady, La Flaca (the Skinny Girl) and even La Madrina (The Godmother), she is the centerpiece of one of the world's fastest growing religious movements.

La Santa Muerte is often translated as "Saint Death." A more accurate translation is Holy Death or Sacred Death. In worshipping her, you do not worship death, but ask her to protect you so you don't die before your time. You ask for a good death where you die peacefully in old age and in a manner that does not bring shame upon your family. You ask for safe delivery to the afterlife. You ask her for love, prosperity, healing or other miracles.

Roots

She shares similarities with the Aztec Lady of the Dead, Mictecacihuatl, the queen of Mictlan (the underworld). Like La Santa Muerte, Mictecacihuatl was depicted as a defleshed body. She ruled over the afterlife, though not alone. Alongside her was another deity, her husband Mictlantecuhtli.

Though La Calavera Catrina also has her origin in Mictlan's queen, she is not a folk saint. She first appeared as a satirical drawing by cartoon illustrator and lithographer José Guadalupe Posada. Drawing her with a European-styled hat replete with feather plumes, flowers and black netting, Posada aimed to satirize those Mexicans who he felt were ashamed of their roots and trying to adopt European aristocratic conventions.

When artist Diego Rivera incorporated her image into the mural *Sueño de una Tarde Dominical en la Alameda Central* ("Dream of a Sunday afternoon along Central Alameda"), her popularity blossomed.

These days Lady Death, as she is also known, is an icon of the Mexican holiday known as the Dia de los Muertos (Day of the Dead), which celebrates the lives of the deceased. In Mexico City, shops sell her statues, which often are part of the festival's processions.

In 2016, federal and local authorities inaugurated a Dia de los Muertos parade in Mexico City. 250,000 people attended. Women with their faces painted as skulls dressed in traditional costume and danced along the parade route.

An unlikely source sparked this reclaiming of cultural identity: The

opening scenes of the James Bond movie *Spectre*, in which James Bond chases a villain through a crowd of people who are watching a parade of people dressed as skeletons.

Though people have worshipped Santa Muerte in Mexico since the 18th century, her worship was private. Shrines were personal, home-made affairs until 2001 when Enriqueta Romero (Doña Queta) erected a life-size statue of the saint on the sidewalk in front of her home in the Tepito barrio. Later (in 2008), Enriqueta inherited her son's 75-foot statue and temple in Tultitlan after her son's murder.

Narco Saint?

The third season of the TV drama series "Breaking Bad" alludes to La Santa Muerte's popularity among Mexican drug traffickers. Hitmen for the Juarez Cartel belly-crawl to her shrine to petition for someone's death. Detractors point to this popularity as evidence of her being a so-called narco saint.

Narco saints are patrons of illegal acts, including drug-dealing. One example is the folk saint Jesus Malverde, a legendary bandit from Sinaloa state. After police killed him in 1909, he became the patron saint of bandits, drug-dealers and other outlaws.

But is The Bony Lady a true narco saint? Though it's true that drug dealers pray to her to protect a shipment of cocaine, they also pray to the Catholic St. Jude Thaddeus, patron saint of lost or difficult causes for similar intercession. That doesn't make St. Jude a narco saint, nor, do her supporters say, does it make her one.

They say her appeal to the narcos is because "Like death, La Santa Muerte does not discriminate." This makes her a perfect saint for the poor, the disenfranchised and the outcast. She has many devotees in prisons. Sex workers pray to her for protection.

Because she is non-judgmental, devotees may ask her for help that traditional saints would be unlikely to give. Some members of the Mexican LGBT community consider her to be their protector and ask her to safeguard them against violence, disease and hatred. They invoke her help in love and she is often a presence at same-sex weddings.

She also lends an ear to those who are not poor, disenfranchised or law-breaking. Like death, La Santa Muerte does not discriminate.

Rituals

Her rituals involve many of the same trappings as Catholicism: statues, rosaries, candles and saint cards. Enriqueta Romero leads a traditional rosary every month at her shrine. Attendance is said to be in the thousands.

Candles play a large part in observances. In grocery stores in the United States, where her worship has followed the flow of immigrants, you can find Santa Muerte votive candles with an image of her on the glass enclosure.

Candle colors correspond to specific requests. White candles are for healing, peace, giving thanks and for consecration. Red candles are for love and passion. Black candles can be used for protection, especially from evil Witchcraft, but also for vengeance, including, in rare cases, death. Other common colors include purple (healing), brown (wisdom) and gold (monetary matters).

Petitioners place offerings such as fruit, flowers or tequila on her shrine as they pray for a request. Some leave cigars, while others blow the smoke from a cigar or cigarette into the face of the statue. Though there have been rumors of some making human sacrifices, this is not considered accurate.

Single women hoping to find a husband or married women wishing to punish a cheating spouse appeal to the aspect of La Santa Muerte dressed in a white wedding dress.

Relationship with other Religions

The Catholic church does not officially recognize the skeleton saint and the Vatican has declared the cult of Santa Muerte as blasphemous. The church holds that since death was defeated with Christ's resurrection, a saint of Death cannot exist.

Some see a commonality in the offerings given to the saint and some African traditional religions. For example, Papa Legba and Baron Samedi enjoy offerings of cigar smoke and alcohol (in their case, rum).

Wiccans may notice that the three most common colors used for asking favors (white, red, black) correspond to the Maid, Mother and Crone. Others may note her association with death as similar to that of the Hindu goddess Kali. Yet there are many on both sides who deny any connection.

Regardless of your current spiritual inclinations, the common wisdom is that you should not approach her lightly. If you promise her something in return for her granting a favor, you must deliver. Some say that if you don't keep your promise, she can take away a loved one.

—MORVEN WESTFIELD

Frazer's Two Laws of Magic
Notes Toward a General Theory of Magic, Part II

TOWARD THE BEGINNING of the third edition of *The Golden Bough* (1911), Sir James George Frazer stated two principles or laws that appear to govern all magical work, whether rituals or spells:

> If we analyse the principles of thought on which magic is based, they will probably be found to resolve themselves into two: first, that like produces like, or that an effect resembles its cause; and, second, that things which have once been in contact with each other continue to act on each other at a distance after the physical contact has been severed. The former principle may be called the **Law of Similarity**, the latter the Law of **Contact or Contagion**. From the first of these principles, namely the Law of Similarity, the magician infers that he can produce any effect he desires merely by imitating it: from the second he infers that whatever he does to a material object will affect equally the person with whom the object was once in contact, whether it formed part of his body or not. Charms based on the Law of Similarity may be called **Homoeopathic or Imitative Magic**. Charms based on the Law of Contact or Contagion may be called **Contagious Magic**... Homoeopathic magic is founded on the association of ideas by **similarity**: contagious magic is founded on the association of ideas by contiguity...
>
> Both branches of magic, the homoeopathic and the contagious, may conveniently be comprehended under the general name of Sympathetic Magic, since both assume that things act on each other at a distance through a secret sympathy, the impulse being transmitted from one to the other by means of what we may conceive as a kind of invisible ether, not unlike that which is postulated by modern science for a precisely similar purpose, namely, to explain how things can physically affect each other through a space which appears to be empty.

We may see how these two laws of magic work by looking at an Old English magical ritual that was used a thousand years ago to restore the fertility of fields "if they will not grow well, or if some harmful thing has been done to

them by a sorcerer (*dry*) or by a poisoner (*lyblace*)." Scholars have conveniently titled this ritual *Æcerbot*, or *Field Remedy*. (You can find a complete translation of the ritual online, among the Almanac Extras for this issue.)

Just one old text of this ritual has come down to our time, though faint echoes of it may still be found here and there in modern rural folklore. The only known manuscript of it was written in Old English by a skillful scribe a thousand years ago. He had copied it from an even older manuscript now lost.

The *Æcerbot* ritual is long and complicated. It probably took two days to complete. To work it fully, more than a half-dozen people had to cooperate: (1) the ritualist; (2) a mass-priest (*mæssepreost*) to sing four masses; (3) the man who owns "that land" (*þæt land*), namely, the land on which lie all the many fields (*æceras*) the ritual is meant to protect; (4) several "almsmen" (*ælmesmenn*); (5) a plowman; and somewhere offstage, (6) a baker, who must bake a loaf from special ingredients. It is the land-owner who pays the other participants in the ritual for their parts in the work; but he, too, has his own part to play in the ritual.

The ritualist (or magician, if you like) does most of the work. Since he needs the cooperation of an ordained priest to sing four masses, he is not a priest himself. Yet he does know how to read and write in Latin and in Old English, and he also knows how to intone or sing various Christian ritual texts in Latin. He is, therefore, almost certainly a cleric in what are called the minor orders (such as a lector or an exorcist).

Yet the *Æcerbot* ritual is unconventional and overtly magical. It is not found in any of the standard service books of the Medieval Church. Also, the ritual includes a long versified prayer in Old English, which is framed in old-fashioned poetic diction that was rooted in bygone Pagan times. It is a remarkably ambiguous prayer. Except for one or two words, either a Pagan or a Christian could easily pray it.

The First Day's Work: Contiguity

The ritualist begins his work at night, before daybreak. He cuts out four pieces of green turf (four "turfs"), one from each of the four sides of the land-owner's land. Next he takes four liquids: oil, honey, barm (a product of fermentation that contains live yeast) and milk from all cattle that graze on that land. He also takes some of every kind of tree growing on the land except hard wood and some of every kind of herb except *glappan* (a plant that makes burrs, maybe burdock). He adds holy water to this mix of liquids and plant matter. Then he squeezes the fluid out of this mix onto the bottom of each of the four turfs. He says certain Christian texts of ritual power in Latin over each turf. Among them is the Divine command, *Be fruitful and multiply, and replenish the Earth* (Genesis 1:28 and on a second occasion, Genesis 9:1).

Next he takes the four turfs to the local church and he places them so the green part (upper surface) of each turf faces the altar. Then the mass-priest sings four masses—in Latin, of course—over the four turfs. Singing four masses, as they were commonly sung in the early Middle Ages, will take up much of the mass-priest's day.

While the priest sings these masses, the ritualist is otherwise occupied. He makes four wooden crosses from wood of the tree called quick-beam (*cwicbeame*), probably rowan. (The striking red berries of the rowan tree are used even today to protect from malevolent magic.) On each cross he writes the names of the four Evangelists in Latin, probably one name on each of its four arms. He puts one of these crosses in the bottom of each hole, saying in Latin, *Cross Matthew, Cross Mark, Cross Luke and Cross St. John*.

When the mass-priest has finished singing the four masses, late in the day, the ritualist takes the four turfs back to the same holes from which he dug them. He puts each turf back into its proper hole, saying several Christian texts of ritual power in Latin, repeating these texts nine times over each of the four turfs.

Then the ritualist turns to the east, bows low nine times and says the first thirteen lines of the Old English prayer. Next he turns himself round about three times sunwise or deosil. Then he prostrates himself at full length on the ground and says more Christian texts of

ritual power in Latin. Finally he stands up, stretches out his arms and sings yet more Christian texts of ritual power in Latin. Among them is the *Benedicite*, a very long text from the Bible in which all the creatures of the natural world—among them, the earth and "all things that grow on the earth"—are commanded, each in its turn, to bless their Creator. (In Catholic Bibles, this prayer is Daniel 3:57-88. Protestant Bibles relegate it to the *Apocrypha*, where it is part of *The Song of the Three Holy Children*, verses 35-66; or they omit it altogther.)

All this is to be done, so the manuscript says, for the praise and glory of Christ and Mary and the Cross—but also for the honor of the land-owner and all who are subject to him.

The ritualist has to take care that all this complicated ritual work is finished by sunset. This, however, is just the first half of the ritual. The second half will need to be done on the following day. Before describing the second day's work, however, let us pause to notice something quite distinctive about the first half of the ritual. The magic that has been done up to this point is *a magic that relies heavily on physical contact*. At every step of the way it requires direct physical contact with the land or with the four turfs cut from it, or at least close proximity to them. In other words, this magic is all about **contiguity**. Thus it works almost exclusively with Frazer's **Law of Contact.**

Moreover, the first half of the ritual is heavily tinctured with Christian words in Latin and Christian symbols. One might even call it a piece of *Christian magic*. (The same might be said of many other minor Medieval Christian rituals of blessing, healing and exorcism. These other rituals, like the first half of the *Æcerbot*, also rely far more on contiguity than on **similarity** in their magical actions.)

In very sharp contrast, the work of the second day relies heavily on Frazer's other law, the **Law of Similarity**. Also, it has hardly anything in it that is unambiguously Christian, just a small use of holy water by a baker off-site and a few words of power in Latin from the ritualist at the very end of the second day's work.

The Second Day's Work: Similarity

On the next day, probably in the early morning, the ritualist and the land-owner meet at one of the various fields on the land. The land-owner has already gotten all his plowing gear and tackle (*sulhge-teogo*) together and brought it with him to the field.

The "almsmen" are already there at the field, too. Most likely they are not wandering beggars, but local lads who have come to the field expecting to receive alms from the land-owner. They already know their part in the ritual, for they have brought with them something that wandering beggars seem unlikely to carry in their packs, namely, "uncooth seed" (*uncuþ sæd*), whatever that might be precisely. (No one knows for sure.) The land-owner takes this "uncooth seed" from the almsmen and gives them twice as much in return. (It is not clear exactly how "twice as much" worked in practice, whether the almsmen were given twice as much seed, or—more likely—twice the value of the seed in some other form, such as money or ale.)

The land-owner then puts four things into a hole that has just been bored in the beam of the plow: incense, fennel, hallowed soap and hallowed salt. He then places the "uncooth seed" onto the body of the plow, that is, onto the part that will penetrate the earth and turn the furrow. Then the ritualist speaks the next sixteen lines of the Old English prayer. Thereupon the land-owner (or perhaps a plowman acting for him) "drives forth the plow and starts the first furrow." While this is happening, the ritualist speaks three more lines of the Old English prayer.

Hours before all this was done, probably early in the dawning, a baker had baked a unique loaf of fresh bread "as big as will lie in the hand." The peculiar dough used for this unique loaf was made from every kind of meal that is grown on the land, kneaded together with milk and also with holy water. This unique loaf has already been brought to the field. Now it is put *into* the earth *under* the newly opened first furrow. Then the ritualist says the last six lines of the Old English prayer. (You can read the entire Old English prayer in translation on-line, among the *Almanac Extras* for this issue.)

After everything else has been done, the ritualist repeats three times a few of the Christian words of power in Latin that had already been said on the first day.

With that, the ritual has come to its end and everyone leaves—except, presumably, the plowman, who will work at plowing the land-owner's fields all the day long.

We probably do not need to specify in every small detail just how the Law of Similarity works in the second half of the *Æcerbot* ritual. The symbolism of the plow and the seed, the newly opened furrow in the field and the fresh loaf put into the earth, is unabashedly sexual. And this same symbolism can be heard even now in old-fashioned speech. A man is sometimes still said to *plow* a woman in sexual intercourse and a pregnant woman is sometimes still said to have a loaf in her oven or underneath her apron. Moreover, the three lines of the Old English prayer that the ritualist recites just after the plow penetrates the earth are explicit, even blunt:

Wassail, Earth, Mother of Mankind!
Be fruitful in God's embracing arm,

Be filled with food for the needs of Mankind!

In this context, "embracing arm" is not just a warm and fuzzy metaphor for loving kindness. The image is meant to be openly sexual: the Earth who is embraced is called the Mother of Mankind here, and elsewhere in the ritual the God who embraces her is called Father. Here, too, the Old English word for Earth is not the common word (*eorðe*), but an uncommon, archaic word (*folde*), which seems to be used elsewhere *only* in ritual or magical or poetic diction.

There are also other differences between the two halves of the *Æcerbot* ritual. Apart from the ritualist, the other actors in its second half are all layfolk; but in its first half only a cleric is present to assist the ritualist. The first half is full of Latin texts taken from the Bible and Catholic worship, which amplify the ritual's **coefficient of weirdness** on the first day. (See the first of these *Notes Toward a General Theory of Magic*, in last year's *Witches' Almanac*, page.86) Apart from a few brief Christian words of power at the very end of the work, the second half of the ritual uses no Latin at all. Rather, its **coefficient of weirdness** is provided by the archaic, ritualistic, poetic diction of the Old English prayer.

It seems likely, therefore, that the two halves of the *Æcerbot* ritual arose in different eras and were artificially joined together by a Christian cleric sometime not too long before our sole surviving manuscript was copied. There actually are faint echoes of each half of the *Æcerbot* in modern British folklore, but every one of these folkloric echoes reflects only the first half or only the second half alone, never both halves together.

The first half is echoed by an obscure ritual that used to be carried out in the Parish of Todenham, Gloucestershire. Each year at Rogationtide a procession from the Church traces out the boundary of the Parish, halting at various traditional points on the route. The procession includes four men, each carrying a spade, who were called the "cross-diggers." At each point where the procession halts by tradition, these four men cut a cross-shaped hole into the earth. They make a small mound at the very center of that cross-shaped hole, using the soil they dug up. Then a small green plant is set into the earth at the center of that mound and the procession moves on to the next traditional halting-place.

And the second half finds a parallel in the occasional custom of plowmen to drop a bit of their own noon meal into the first furrow that they cut into a new field.

Looking Forward

Here we end the second of these *Notes Toward a General Theory of Magic*. The third Note should appear in next year's issue of *The Witches' Almanac*. It will connect Frazer's two Laws of Magic with the two principal dimensions of human language and indeed of all symbolic activity. These two dimensions are the very warp and woof of the loom, so to speak, on which humankind naturally weaves all its magic, its spells and rituals alike.

—ROBERT MATHIESEN

✒ Astrological Plant Remedies ✒

THE QUEST FOR WELLNESS of both the mind and body has been linked to astrology through herbal cures related to the Sun, Moon, planets and zodiac signs for thousands of years. A flair for healing, especially with natural remedies, has also long been a focus of those who heed and follow the Old Ways. This approach to wellness, using home remedies with natural and alternative health care, has long been the first choice in maintaining good health in Europe and other parts of the world. This philosophy is rapidly catching on in the United States. With the health care crisis spiraling further out of control it is becoming more and more difficult (often impossible) for Americans to navigate the health care conundrum. Even if we do manage to see an allopathic doctor, the expensive co-pays for consultations and prescriptions can still place health care out of reach.

Preparing herbal teas from wild plants, many easily grown at home or even gathered by the wayside, will often provide an affordable and effective way to maintain good health. Weeds in the eyes of many, but with magical healing potentials for enhancing daily life in the opinions of others, herbal tea blends are an easy and pleasant way to access nature's precious healing powers.

Plants evolve around us, attuning to survive in the world's changing climate and other living conditions. These few inexpensive and easily obtained plants contain at least 60 active ingredients altogether and can be used to create a variety of remedies to address the three facets of healing—mental, physical and emotional. If not found growing wild they can be cultivated in home gardens or purchased at health food stores.

Unless otherwise noted use the plant's leafy parts. Add the herbs to boiling water and allow to steep for 5 to 10 minutes before drinking. About a generous tablespoon of the blended herbs per cup of water usually works well. Use no more than 4 to 5 different herbs per blend to avoid conflicting mixes because herbs are quite powerful. There can be some confusion when first starting to use herbal remedies as many do appear similar, so the Latin names of the plants are listed to aid in selecting the proper herbs. In the case of florals, of course, use the flowers of the plant in question.

There are four steps in assembling your own herbal cures.

1. Choose one base herb. This matrix will be ½ of the blend. This can be green or black table tea, or for a caffeine free blend, nettle, alfalfa, chamomile, raspberry leaf or lemon balm (melissa).

2. Choose one aromatic. This is medicinal and will set the taste as well as the aroma. It should be about ¼ of the blend.

3. Choose one action herb. This creates the major impact or medicinal effectiveness of the tea. This should also be about ¼ of the blend.

4. Finally select a floral (usually chamomile, elder, rose or marigold) and add just a sprinkle for color and subtlety.

Leave the herbs as whole and natural as possible until ready for use. Over-processing or crushing them will lessen their effectiveness. Fresh herbs are good, but wash them well and spread them on trays to dry. A dash of white vinegar in the rinse water will guard against spoilage and bacteria. If doing your own wild crafting observe the plants. Does one seem to be calling you? Listen to your hunches. This can be significant, as that plant's properties might be exactly what are needed at the present time. Astrologers can also consider which body parts correlate with the planetary rulers listed to aid in selecting the best plants to address a given wellness issue.

Herbs to Blend For Teas

Yarrow—*Achillea Millefolium* (Venus) Action; Reduces fevers, lowers blood pressure, and stabilizes the hormonal cycle. It is also a liver tonic and anti-inflammatory.

Dog Rose—*Rosa Canina* (Venus) Floral; Decorative but also Action; Helps acute respiratory problems and herpes. Demulcent, astringent.

Lavender—*Lavendula Agustifolia* (Mercury) Aromatic; An anti-microbial sedative that quells anxiety and fosters a positive mental outlook. As a sachet lavender is used magically to draw friends.

Sage—*Salvia Officinalis* (Jupiter) Aromatic; Longevity-boosting and filled with antioxidants, sage is used for sore throat and digestive upsets. The phrase "old sage" hints at the life extension properties sage is credited with. Also it can be burned as a smudge or incense to clear away negative energies.

Nettle—*Urtica Dioic* (Mars) Base or Action; A nourishing cleanser and detoxifier used for anemia and allergies. The soup makes an excellent healthy meal. Use the whole plant and add the vegetables of your choice. Nettle soup is especially popular in Ireland.

Rosemary—*Rosemarinus Officinalis* (Sun) Action or Aromatic; A memory aid that relieves headaches, rejuvenates and energizes. Rosemary is thought to beautify the speaking or singing voice. It also makes an excellent hair rinse. Try mixing it with vinegar to use on dark hair.

Raspberry leaf—*Rubus Idaeus* (Venus) Base; Raspberry aids digestion and eases female complaints.

Thyme—*Thymus Vulgaris* (Venus) Aromatic; Anti-viral and great for sore throats, sinuses and coughs. Magically thyme is carried as a sachet to connect with the elementals, fairies, elves, etc.

Marigold—*Calendula Officinalis* (Sun) Floral; Detoxifying, anti-microbial and used for both skin troubles and stomach upsets. Marigold is best gathered in the afternoon after a day in the bright sunlight.

Mugwort—*Artemis Vulgaris* (Venus and Moon) Action; Stimulates the liver, purges worms and dissolves fat. Mugwort is famous for enhancing dreams and aiding in psychic dream work when used as a tea or sachet.

Meadowsweet—*Filipendula Ulmaria* (Jupiter) Action; Relieves overall pain and has an aspirin-like effect.

Peppermint—*Mentha Piperita* (Mars and Venus) Action; Mint has been called the aspirin of the herb world, also mint makes a good table tea all by itself. Relieves pain, nausea, gas and calms nerves to alleviate stress. Often mint is carried as a sachet for general spiritual protection and to offset the negative.

Melissa—*Melissa Officinalis* (Jupiter) Base or Action; This lemony flavored tea base is a wonderful anti-depressant and toothache remedy that treats boils when applied topically to the afflicted area. Sometimes called lemon balm, this base tea is linked to a Lord Llewellyn of Wales who was said to have lived to be over a hundred years old. He credited his longevity to drinking a daily cup of lemon balm tea each morning.

Alfalfa—*Medicago Sativa* (Sun) Base or Action; Body building and a rich source of minerals and vitamins, especially iron. Alfalfa is anti-inflammatory, treating fatigue, allergies, blood disorders and diabetes.

Basil—Ocimum Cum or Ocimum Santum (Mars) Aromatic or Action; Lowers blood pressure, detoxifies, anti-inflammatory. In Hindu temples basil water is often placed in small bowls before deities for the faithful to sip or use as a holy blessing water. This is believed to offer spiritual healing. A live basil plant carefully cultivated as a kitchen herb has also been used to facilitate conception in women who wish to have a child.

Wood Betony—*Stachyus Betonia* (Jupiter) Action; An astringent that treats depression, panic attacks and hysteria.

Chamomile—*Anthemus Nobilis* (Sun) Floral or Base; Calming, relieves insomnia, stomach cramps and colic. This pleasant apple scented tea is often served to children as a nursery tea. Add a dash of lemon juice and use it to prepare a wonderful hair rinse for blonds or red heads.

Cinnamon—*Cinnamomum* (Sun and Jupiter) Aromatic; Use the bark either whole or ground. Kidney and bladder tonic, anti-bacterial, anti-biotic, warming, relieves chills. Spiritually cinnamon is linked to prosperity. A bit sprinkled in one's shoes or wallet before a job interview is said to draw financial opportunities. Place three shiny pennies beneath the front door mat and sprinkle them with cinnamon to draw extra money into the house.

Catnip—*Nepeta Cataria* (Venus) Action or Base; Calming, relieving colds, flu, arthritis and headaches. A sachet of catnip, will delight your feline familiar. Plant it in the garden to attract cats.

Elder—*Sambucus Nigra* (Venus) Floral or Aromatic; Use the berries, flowers or leaves. Treats colds, flu, muscles pains, rheumatism and arthritis, sore throat and fevers. Combines well with mint as a medicinal tea. Elder berry is also used to make table jelly and wine.

Mullein—*Verbascum Thapses* (Saturn) Floral or Action; Use the flowers, root or leaves. One of the oldest remedies, mullein has been used to treat asthma, insomnia, mumps, bowel problems, ulcers and tumors. Crush the flowers and use to remove warts. Also called hag's or witch's taper, mullein is a majestic plant which has been planted or carried to repel evil influences.

Bay Laurel—*Laurus Nobilis* (Sun) Aromatic; Use the bark and berries as well as the leaves. This especially valuable herb is good as a gargle for sore throats, treats bleeding gums, is a stimulant and makes a pleasant digestive tonic. A popular culinary herb, an especially wonderful way to use bay is to add a leaf or two when preparing a pot of rice. In magic, bay laurel leaves are effective in wish fulfillment and prosperity. Write a wish on a small piece of paper and wrap it around the leaf, or add three leaves to a box of coins to draw extra money as needed. Place the leaf or box on your altar.

Marjoram—*Origanum Majorana* (Mercury) Action; Used to treat tonsillitis, colds and gas. Topically apply it as a disinfectant or to treat bruises.

Parsley—*Petroselinum Crispum* (Mars) Aromatic or Action; Treats kidney stones, blood disorders, halitosis and jaundice.

— DIKKI-JO MULLEN

117

Axis Mundi

ONE OF THE MORE common symbols seen in Pagan religious practices today is the tree. Typically, it is an image of a tree that is green and full—a tree as would be seen at the height of summer. The top branches point to the sky above, the roots of the trees anchor it deeply in the fertile earth.

The image of the tree can be seen as a metaphor for many things—our own spiritual development, a link between earth and sky, a practical reminder that we only have one planet and are all equally responsible for its care, or as what is sometimes referred to as the Axis Mundi.

The Axis Mundi or "World Tree" is understood by many to represent a central point or link not only between earth and sky, but the place where the four elemental directions meet. As such, the World Tree can be seen as a place of balance and unity.

Perhaps what makes this metaphor so easy to grasp is the vertical nature of the tree. It grows up and branches out. Every tree, no matter how splendid, starts as a seed. The growth does not occur overnight but across many years. Relating to this image becomes easy when considering our own natural growth process. In mundane terms, we are all born and we all grow up from children to adults. Another layer that may be applied to better understanding the metaphor is the development of personal spiritual paths in our lifetime. As a child we often begin

this journey by assimilating the belief systems of our elders. As adults we have the opportunity to deepen our understanding of these mysteries or perhaps explore new philosophies.

The downstairs/upstairs view of our connection to divinity is shared across many different religious disciplines. Whether considering trees, sacred mountaintops or man-made towers such as minarets and church steeples, the message seems consistent and clear: God (however we define him/her/it) is not "down here" but "up there."

World Trees are a common symbol in the mythical worlds of pre-Columbian cultures such as the Maya. In some villages an actual tree (often the tallest or oldest in the village) is revered as a living example of the Axis Mundi. Landscaping and harvesting is always done around these trees—they are considered to be sacred and are never compromised. It is not uncommon, even in the larger cities of Central and South America, to see these ancient monoliths standing firm and strong in the center of highways and streets, the roads and streets clearly built around them.

In some of the smaller villages, one can still discover community altars beneath the elder tree, a place where offerings are left by the inhabitants of the village. An equal armed cross is sometimes placed on top of the altar. At first glance it would be easy to assume that a Christian influence is at play. But then one remembers the significance of the World Tree as a place where the four cardinal points meet. A place of balance and unity.

The Mayans equate each part of the tree to a specific realm. The earth beneath the tree is the Underworld, a dark place filled with mystery, magic and danger. The souls of the dead reside there and although the living may follow the roots downward into the earth to commune with their ancestors, it is not always easy to find one's way back to the surface. The lower half of the tree is a place for the living. Birds and monkeys inhabit its dense foliage. Adults take shelter and enjoy shade beneath the tree and children play in the lower branches. The top half of the tree reaches the Heavens and is the World of the Gods.

As ambitious as men can be in their quest to touch divinity, there is a point between Earth and Sky where humans are ill-advised to travel while still in their physical incarnations. The monkeys and birds on the other hand have immunity. They can travel to the very top of the tree and return safely again to the ground below. These animals are sacred because in this context they are believed to be the messengers of the Gods, gentle emissaries that can move freely from one realm to another and back again.

Beautiful and powerful imagery to be sure, but perhaps the most profound image is the sky that arches above the Tree—a sky filled with golden light during the day and painted with brilliant stars each night. A sky that reminds us that as long as we are alive we can aspire to go higher and higher in our personal journey toward enlightenment.

—JIMAHL DI FIOSA

IMAGO TYPHONIS
IVXTA APOLLODORVM.

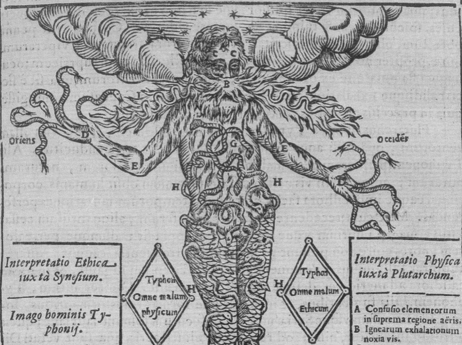

Interpretatio Ethica iuxtà Synesium.

Imago hominis Typhonij.

A Confusio mentis seu intellectus.
B Æstus concupiscentiæ.
C Libido & lingua virulenta.
D Opera mala.
E Leuitas mentis, & iactabunda ostentatio.
G Hypocrisis
H Inuidiæ rabies per serpentes.
I Ira & furor animi.
K Inconstantia & lubricitas mentis.

Typhon Omne malum physicum
Typhon Omne malum Ethicum

Interpretatio Physica iuxtà Plutarchum.

A Confusio elementorum in suprema regione aëris.
B Ignearum exhalationum noxia vis.
C Ardor Martius omnia adurens.
D Vis noxia omnes Mundi partes peruadens.
E Celeritas ventorum Typhonicorum.
G Perturbatio aëris per noxias ventorum qualitates.
H Corruptio aëris ex pernitiosis ventorum flatibus.
I Fulminis, tonitruum, & fulguris eius.
K Montibus, & mari maximè dominantur venti.

Terribilis postquam Iunonis creuit Alumnus
Anguineis pedibus, sublimi vertice cœlum
Tangebat, corpus plumæ anguesque tegebant
Innumeri, plagas orientis dextera Soli
Cùm staret, plagas tangebat læua cadentis,
His centum capita expirantia naribus ignem,
Ausa Iouem contra, cœlumque insurgere contra.

Merry Meetings

A candle in the window, a fire on the hearth,
a discourse over tea…

IN AN ERA REPLETE with magical innovation Jason Miller's approach stands taller than many. Strategic Sorcery is the name given to his own particular approach to magic which informed by his decades of studying Ceremonial Magic, as well as Folk Magic techniques and Witchcraft. For Jason, each discipline strengthened the other and made for a Sorcery that could be streamlined for the modern world. Below, Jason took some time to share his approach with us.

What was the trigger that set you on a magical path?

When I was five I had a psychic experience on the playground. I looked up from the ground, but looked up beyond reality. Like everything on earth was underneath me. It felt like all space and time was like a painting at my feet. From that moment on I always felt like there was something behind what we could all see and feel — like people moving behind the curtains of a play. That feeling never left me and triggered a bunch of strange experiences that kept up for about a year. Eventually they stopped but the feeling never left, and when I got older I started exploring spirituality and magic.

Tell us about your early magical training.

My first magical teacher was actually a teacher in High School. She bought me my first deck of Tarot cards and taught me how to shield and do some simple Rosicrucian-type stuff. She would look at the books I was reading and give ad-vice. After her, I made some acquaintances at a Conjure Shop called "The Globe" and a Botanica in Lakewood NJ. It turned out that the son of the owner of the Botanica was in the after-school program that I was a counselor at, so I had an in. I started combining Ceremonial Magic stuff that I was reading in Modern Magick and other books with Rootwork and Folk Magic. This also fit nicely into Paul Huson's approach to Witchcraft that he took in Mastering Witchcraft which was a big early influence. I worked from books mostly, but was lucky to have mentors that I could ask questions of. Eventually I met John Myrdhin Reynolds, the first westerner to be ordained as a Ngakpa – a Tantric Sorcerer, and he took a strong interest in me and my development.

I still marvel at the conflux of forces that had to come together for me to meet a Rosicrucian, a Conjure Man, and a Ngakpa: all willing to guide me, all within 20 miles of my house in central NJ, and all before I was 20 years old. Remarkable really. I will always

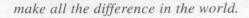

make all the difference in the world.

Tell us a bit about your travels.

There are really only two big trips that I took, but each was for over the course of several months. In 1993 I did the whole "Eurail Backpacking" rite of passage. I started in England and was lucky enough to meet some people connected to the Regency Coven that could present a different view of Witchcraft than was common at the time. More akin to Huson than Gardner. I visited lots of holy places, both Christian and Pagan. I headed to Ireland and got to not only New Grange, but got a local to take me to the Dowth mound which was not open to the public at the time. I also meditated in the Dunmore Cave which is one of the locations rumored to be an entrance to the underworld. After that I started wandering the continent just keeping an eye out and trusting providence to lead me to likeminded people. I met some practitioners of Vampirism in Budapest. Learned to read playing cards on a train from Venice to Berlin. That kind of thing. Nothing very structured. I just wanted to get out and see the places I had read about.

be in all their debt as well as the debt of many other teachers I have learned from since.

What advice would you give the beginner in this day and has your opinion evolved over time?

Take advantage of the immense amount of access that you have. Back in the 80's and early 90's we had plenty of books, but nothing like what there is today, and certainly no ability to instantly connect with likeminded people. Some things are lost because of it and certainly people can get lost in their filter bubble, but it's overall a good thing.

Beyond that I would say that no matter what tradition you follow, make sure that you are meditating and making offerings. These two things are not part of every tradition, and they are often neglected, but they can

In the late 90s I had been studying Tantra for a few years and wanted to go to Nepal for a while to deepen my studies. In 1999 I headed to Nepal and lived for a month with Kunzang Dorje, one of the greatest Tantric Magicians of the age. I then got an apartment in Boudhanath where I studied Dzogchen and Tibetan Magic with John Reynolds (Lama Vanranatha) who I have known since I was a teenager, as well as many other La-

mas: most notably Moktsa Rinpoche and Lopon Tenzin Namdak. I stayed in Nepal through the spring of 2000 and came home after receiving signs that I should return to the west and apply what I had learned in the east, back into my Western occult training.

How much has Eastern thought informed your daily practice?

A massive amount. Even though I don't often teach on Tantric topics directly the manner in which meditation, ceremonial magic, folk magic and energy work combine seamlessly to make a potent system is something that informs everything I do. Indeed, the teachings in my Sorcery of Hekate course were only possible because of my eastern training.

You call your particular approach to magic "Strategic Sorcery." How is it different from Ceremonial Magic and/ or Witchcraft?

Well let's take the Sorcery part first. I use that term for two reasons. The first is precisely that it is not Ceremonial Magic or Witchcraft. It's something in between. It's also purely operative and speaks to someone doing magic meant to make changes in the world. It is possible to call yourself a magician but be concerned only with spiritual growth. It is possible to be a Witch and be concerned only with religious celebration. There is no mistaking the Sorcerer—he is there to cast spells and mess around with minds and events.

The Strategic part comes from my approach to the art. I don't just believe in doing magic then following it up with

mundane actions – I believe in the strategic melding of the two. One informs the other at every stage of the game until you reach your goals. A lot of people out there are perfectly capable at spells and magic, but apply it in ways that are counter-productive and shortsighted. Strategic Sorcery is the answer to that.

It's public knowledge that you had a transformative experience around Hecate while traveling in the far east, without going into the details that are intimate, can you tell us a little about it?

Yes absolutely. I had been sent by Kunzang Dorje Rinpoche to the charnel ground of Pashupatinath where I was supposed to meditate on my own impermanence. Pashupatinath is on the Bhaghamati River and is like Varnassi in India, in that they perform open air cremations on the ghats, *platforms that line the river. On the third day of meditating on the cremations I had a vision of a woman in saffron robe that was more Greek*

in style than Tibetan or Nepalese. I knew somehow it was Hekate and when I objected that I was doing something else she told me that all charnel grounds are hers. She told me to go to the wilderness when I got back to the States and offer her a supper of Eggs and Honey at a three way crossroads.

When I returned to NJ, I went to the Pine Barrens and that is exactly what I did. That was the beginning of a teaching that has taken 13 years to receive and process. The system that I now teach in my Sorcery of Hekate training.

Much of your written work seems to focus on individual work, is there a "lodge" or "group" equivalent?

I am all for people working in groups and there are now a few Strategic Sorcery groups out there that work together, but there is no Lodge in the sense of the OTO or Golden Dawn. I am not one much for degrees and titles and I always learned best from individuals rather than groups. In a sense the entire Strategic Sorcery community (now over 1400 people!) is a group in that we perform global rites that are linked by doing them the same way at the same time. A "meeting in the air" as they say.

Much of your work is quite innovative, where will it be in 5, 10 or 20 years?

Oh who can say? I am launching a new course this week on Sorcery for Entrepreneurs. I am very passionate about financial magic and getting Pagans

and Magicians to take their finances on as part of their path, rather than something that they avoid or think of as inherently unspiritual. In five years I hope that it and the other courses are still flourishing and that I am still learning new things.

In ten years I hope to be traveling a bit more as my kids will be almost grown. I would like to start giving weekend and week-long retreats at that point where we can go deep into immersive practice and learning.

In 20 years I will be 64, and like Ringo says "Will you still need me, will you still feed me, when I'm 64?" I hope so. I would love to be traveling more with my wife and scaling back my active teaching at that point so that I am mostly answering questions and commenting on the teachings I have already produced. That is as close to retirement as I want to get. I hope to still be in the game and still relevant.

A list of Jason Miller's books can be found on our website at TheWitchesAlmanac.com

☯HE ART OF ☯EOMANCY

Geomancy is an ancient system of divination that uses sixteen symbols or figures. Easy to learn and use, it was one of the most popular divination methods in the Middle Ages and Renaissance, remaining in use among rural cunning folk for centuries thereafter. Though it's been neglected in recent times, geomancy still has much to offer and has begun a renaissance of its own in the last few years.

The sixteen geomantic figures are made up of single and double points. Each has a name and divinatory meaning, and is also assigned to one of the four Elements, twelve signs of the Zodiac and seven Planets or the nodes of the Moon.

The first figure is PUER (pronounced POO-er) which means "boy." It represents masculine energy. It is favorable in love and in conflict or competition. Its element is Fire, its sign is Aries and its planet is Mars.

The second figure is AMISSIO (ah-MISH-yo) which means "loss." It represents losing something and is favorable for love (losing your heart) and health questions (losing an illness). Its element is Earth, its sign is Taurus and its planet is Venus.

The third figure is ALBUS (AHL-buss) which means "white." It represents peace. It is favorable for learning and profit. Its element is Air, its sign is Gemini and its planet is Mercury.

The fourth figure is POPULUS (POP-oo-loose) which means "crowd." It represents society. It is passive and unstable. Its element is Water, its sign is Cancer and its planet is the waxing Moon.

The fifth figure is FORTUNA MAJOR (for-TOO-na MAY-or) which means "greater fortune." It represents power and is favorable in all questions. Its element is Fire, its sign is Leo and its planet is the Sun in spring and summer.

The sixth figure is CONJUNCTIO (con-YOONK-sho) which means "joining." It represents meeting and is favorable for love and gain. Its element is Earth, its sign Virgo and its planet Mercury.

The seventh figure is PUELLA (poo-ELL-a) which means "girl." It represents feminine energy. It is favorable for love and the arts. Its element is Air, its sign Libra and its planet Venus.

The eighth figure is RUBEUS (roo-BAY-us) which means "red." It represents passion and is favorable for violence. Its element is Water, its sign Scorpio and its planet Mars.

The ninth figure is ACQUISITIO (AK-wi-SISH-yo) which means "gain" and represents acquiring

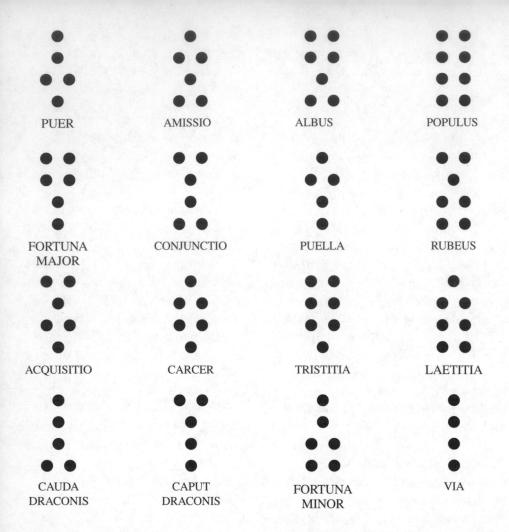

PUER AMISSIO ALBUS POPULUS

FORTUNA MAJOR CONJUNCTIO PUELLA RUBEUS

ACQUISITIO CARCER TRISTITIA LAETITIA

CAUDA DRACONIS CAPUT DRACONIS FORTUNA MINOR VIA

something. It is favorable except when you want to lose something. Its element is Fire, its sign Sagittarius and its planet Jupiter.

The tenth figure is CARCER (CAR-ser) which means "prison." It represents limitation. It is only favorable for restriction. Its element is Earth, its sign Capricorn and its planet Saturn.

The eleventh figure is TRISTITIA (triss-TISH-a) which means "sorrow." It represents downward movement. It is favorable only for stability and

security. Its element is Air, its sign Aquarius and its planet Saturn.

The twelfth figure is LAETITIA (leh-TISH-a) which means "joy." It represents upward movement. It is favorable for all questions except when secrets need to be kept. Its element is Water, its sign Pisces and its planet Jupiter.

The thirteenth figure is CAUDA DRACONIS (COW-da dra-CON-iss) which means "dragon's tail." It represents ending. It is favorable only for ending something. Its element is

Fire and it stands for the south node of the Moon.

The fourteenth figure is CAPUT DRACONIS (CAH-poot dra-CON-iss) which means "dragon's head." It represents beginnings and is favorable for starting anything. Its element is Earth and it stands for the north node of the Moon.

The fifteenth figure is FORTUNA MINOR (for-TOO-na MEE-nor) which means "lesser fortune." It represents speed and is favorable for anything swift. Its element is Air, its sign Leo and its planet the Sun in autumn and winter.

The sixteenth and last figure is VIA (VEE-ah) which means "road." It represents change and is favorable for journeys and changes. Its element is Water, its sign Cancer and its planet the waning Moon.

To cast a geomantic reading, all you need is some way to get an odd or even number. A flipped coin will do the trick, as will ordinary dice, a pack of playing cards or any other random method. One quick way to get a geomantic figure is to toss a quarter, a dime, a nickel and a penny. Heads are a single point, tails a double point, and the coins are the four lines—the quarter is the top, the dime the second, the nickel the third and the penny the bottom line. With any other method, an odd number gives a single point, an even number a double point.

A full geomantic reading casts four figures and then combines them in various ways to make eleven more. However, a simple reading can be done by casting two figures and adding them together to make a third. Toss your coins or use whatever other method you choose. Copy down the results as a figure and then repeat the process, copying the second figure to the left of the first. (Geomancy always goes from right to left.) Then add each line of the two figures. Two single points or two double points gives you a double point; one single plus one double gives you a single point. Copy the third figure below and between the first two. The first figure you cast represents you, the second figure is the situation, and the third figure is the outcome.

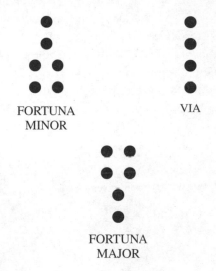

FORTUNA MINOR   VIA

FORTUNA MAJOR

Here, for example, the first toss of the coins was heads, heads, tails, tails, and the second was all heads; giving the two figures Fortuna Minor and Via. Add them together and the result is Fortuna Major. The person who cast the reading hopes to achieve something quickly (Fortuna Minor), and given a willingness to embrace change (Via), success (Fortuna Major) is on its way.

—JOHN MICHAEL GREER

GREAT MULLEIN

The Witch's Taper

IN THE REALMS of Witchcraft and herbal medicine, few herbs are as well-used and well-loved as mullein (*Verbascum thapsus*.) An Old World plant found in most Medieval and Renaissance pharmacopeias, mullein was eventually brought to Australia and North America by European colonists, and was spread throughout US territories by no less a plant authority than "Johnny Appleseed" Chapman himself.

This easily-identifiable plant grows in a biennial cycle. In its first year of life, after months spent transforming underground through the winter cold, the plant first emerges in the springtime as an almost cabbage-like rosette of broad, fuzzy, pale green leaves. By its second spring, a tall stalk appears and climbs upwards, covered in small, green, cubic purses which eventually develop into the soft petals of yellow flowers. Certain plants can sprout multiple, tentacle-like stalks which curve toward the sky. Though most specimens won't grow more than four or five feet in height,

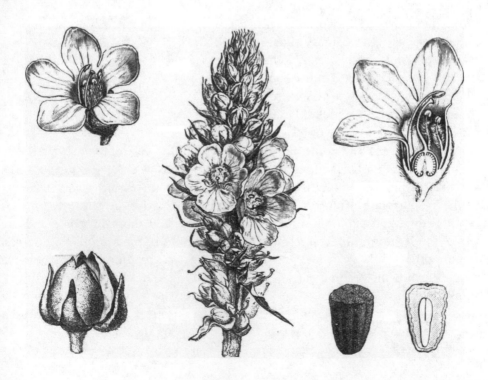

some exceptional plants can grow upwards of ten feet or more. It is said that seeds of the plant can remain dormant for decades—some studies claim over a century—and still be ready to germinate when conditions are right.

Medicinally, Mullein is used for a variety of lung and skin disorders. Both its inhaled smoke and a tea made from its leaves and flowers are said to help ease asthma and bronchitis symptoms, as well as aid general lung function, while an oil made by infusing the fresh flowers can be used to fight ear infections. For those hiking and in a bit of a pinch, one will be hard-pressed to find larger, more velvety leaves than those from the lower portion of a Mullein plant, should nature call at an inconvenient time.

Some nicknames of Mullein are "Hag Tallow" or "Witch's Taper," due to the herb's centuries-old use as a makeshift torch in the days before flashlights and electricity. After the second-year stalks died and dried out, many country folk—typically thrifty widows and wise women who preferred to not spend funds on more expensive light sources—would gather and soak the tops in oil, lighting them when needed, providing the perfect temporary illumination for a nighttime walk or herb-gathering session.

Mullein is most commonly found along roadsides and pathways, highways and overgrown spaces. In this way, it is a powerful ally for hedge magic and crooked path sorcery, thriving at crossroads, in graveyards and other places which represent the intersection of society and wild nature. Astrologically ruled by the planet Saturn, certain grimoires claim it to be highly pleasant to the spirits of the dead, with the dried leaves even capable of being substituted for graveyard dirt in certain conjurations, or burned in incense blends dedicated to sciomantic rites.

—ANTHONY TETH

Sigil Witchery

A SIGIL IS A SYMBOL, sign or design that is believed to have magickal properties. It can be carved, drawn, painted or inked on to any surface such as metal, clay, paper or skin. It does not have to make sense to anyone else who may see it as long as it holds meaning for the person who crafts and uses it.

What can you use a sigil for? It can be a mark of ownership, a symbol of protection, an aid in healing, a beacon for guidance, a tool for meditation, a call sign for deity, spirit and so forth. A sigil embodies a larger complex idea into a simplified image—essentially a kind of metaphysical shorthand!

Although certain magickal systems have evolved complex ways of making sigils, I would argue that sigilcraft is one of the oldest and simplest forms of magick, accessible to anyone willing to pick up a pen, pencil or brush. Lines, markings and carefully engraved designs on rocks, bones and shells found in ancient caves signify the start of humanity's capacity to picture time and space—to tell stories and mark ownership or clan. Our ancestors believed those simple lines, patterns and shapes had power. Thousands upon thousands of years later we still carry this core belief, evident from traffic signs to symbols of faith.

Visual artists who have been trained to interpret the world by translating it into lines, marks, shapes and colors, may find it very intuitive to carry those same skills into spellcraft and specifically the crafting of sigils. The right brain is known for seeing and understanding the world of images, and many of our most instinctual traits are also lodged in this realm. These skills also include visualization—a key tool for working magick. So whether you're more of a visual person or find you often get bogged down in analytical details and words, this approach may work exceedingly well for you.

Sigil witchery is not difficult to learn and is incredibly satisfying and useful. Essentially all you need is a basic understanding of magick and a way to make your sigil. So if you understand how to focus your intent and have some paper and a pen, you're well on your way.

To start, consider what it is you want to manifest. With what key words or phrases can you express it? Write down a short list that describes what you wish to accomplish. Next, consider what shapes and symbols have meaning for you. For example, what does a horizontal line mean to you? An arrow, star, circle, triangle or square? What about a heart or a spiral? Your astrological sign or the phases of the Moon? Do certain colors have personal meaning for you?

Now look at the list of words you have written and consider what shapes and marks can represent them. It is often best to start with the word that represents the key idea and put that shape down first. Then consider the rest of the words and their corresponding shapes, using them to build upon the base shape. If a shape or mark doesn't make sense you can erase it or start again, allowing yourself to brainstorm through the process.

Many work out sigils with a ball point pen, creating a worksheet for each. That way one can evaluate all of the designs made once they're done, instead of getting bogged down with overthinking each mark. The most important thing is that you are putting pen to paper, activating the eye-hand-brain coordination that helps you remember better than anything you could type or digitally create. The page should also have the word list, the date and who the sigil is for, if creating them for other people.

Once you have finalized your sigil, it's time to put it to use! You can mark your cubicle with it on a post-it note or marker it underneath your chair. It can be etched onto a talisman necklace. The sigil can be drawn with chalk on the floor or painted on a wall. You can tattoo it or burn a marked paper in a cauldron. You can design a complex ritual around it or just start using it. Where, how and when all depend on what works best for your purpose.

The most important thing in sigil crafting is finding a method that works best for you. We've been creating symbols and giving them power since the dawn of humanity, so there's a lot of options and variations. Allow yourself some room to practice and you'll be making your own marks in no time!

—LAURA TEMPEST ZAKROFF

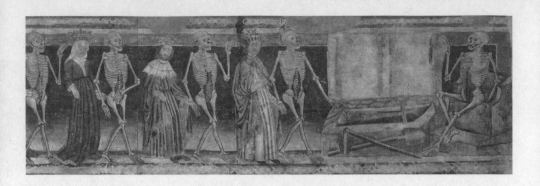

COFFIN RINGS

MEMENTO MORI, Latin for "remember that you must die," refers to a practice of reflecting on death and mortality. It's an admonition to seize the day and not fritter away your existence on things that do not matter.

One also contemplates the lives of others. Not only is your own life fleeting, but also the lives of those we love. Too soon they are gone, yet we should keep them in our thoughts. From this desire springs memento jewelry.

One example from the early 1700s is the coffin ring. Taking its name from the coffin-shaped crystal at the top, the ring was a gold band with a skeleton inlaid in black enamel. Around the ring there might be other symbols of death: a pick and shovel, a crown to indicate that death is the master of all, a tablet upon which the words "memento mori" have been inscribed.

Under the coffin-shaped crystal, which was mounted in line with the band, would be a tiny painted gold skeleton on a black background. Sometimes a single strand of the deceased's hair would be placed between the skeleton and the crystal. In an early example of a coffin ring, the face of the crystal was carved in the shape of a skull.

In England, memento mori jewelry enjoyed a revival during the reign of Queen Victoria (1837–1901).

She lost her mother and then her beloved husband Prince Albert in the same year (1861). When the Queen mourned, the country mourned, and followed her expressions of grief when mourning their own losses. In America, the mourning jewelry trend experienced its height in popularity after the Civil War, which ended by proclamation in 1865.

Coffin rings today often contain a stone, but it's much larger and mounted across the band. Instead of a clear crystal, you're more likely to find a precious or semi-precious stone. Ruby, emerald and onyx are common. Those without stones are often similar to poison rings; that is, they have a compartment that would have been used in the sixteenth century to hold poison.

Though we remember that nefarious use for the compartment, it was also used for holding locks of hair, messages and even tiny portraits of a loved one. When this compartment was made in the shape of a coffin, the ring was referred to as a funeral ring.

Slim band or large fashion accessory, the coffin ring reminds us of the universality of death, and of our loved ones, whether living or beyond the veil.

—MORVEN WESTFIELD

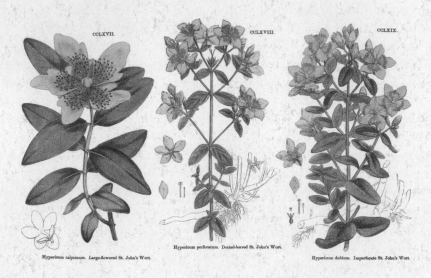

CCLXVII. CCLXVIII. CCLXIX.

Hypericum calycinum. Large-flowered St. John's Wort.   Hypericum perforatum. Dotted-leaved St. John's Wort.   Hypericum dubium. Imperforate St. John's Wort.

ST. JOHN'S WORT

THE LEGENDARY POWERS of the bright yellow herb known as St. John's Wort date back at least as far as medieval times when it was believed to influence anyone opposing the will of a Witch. Ignorant of its true use but aware of its power, the tormentors of Witches in those days held the plant to the mouths of those accused of malevolence to make them confess. It is interesting to speculate whether the presence of the sacred herb might have enabled a genuine Witch to turn the tables and go free.

Originally called Fuga Daemonum (flight of demons), the plant was accorded respect as providing protection against the force of evil thoughts. Irish folklore records the custom of carrying a bit of the plant under the left armpit as an amulet of protection.

St. John's Wort was traditionally gathered before sunrise on the day of Midsummer Eve. Any remaining dew on the petals was carefully collected in small vials to be used as an eye lotion through the coming year. That night, bundles of the herb were passed through the purifying smoke of the annual festival fires and bouquets were made to be hung above doors and windows to guard the home against threat of fire, thunderbolts and other dangers. A maiden might place a sprig of the herb beneath her pillow and dream of a future love. And a childless wife, it was said, might end her barrenness if she would pick a spray of the plant while walking naked in her garden on Midsummer Eve.

The bright golden blossoms of St. John's Wort resemble miniature Suns and when infused in oil or alcohol change the color of the liquid to blood red. The petals, if dropped in cold water impart their golden hue to it. The properties and its curious balsamic odor lend the plant an aura of mystery and many customs and legends have grown up about it.

It should be noted that the herb has a place in folk medicine. A balm called red oil (macerate four ounces of the tops of St. John's Wort in olive oil overnight) is still in use as a home remedy for soothing bruises. An infusion of one ounce of the dried herb of St. John in one pint of boiling water, steeped and dosed in wineglassful is said to ease coughs from colds or other lung distress.

But the most significant occult use of St. John's Wort is only hinted at in printed books. The herb has the traditional power to protect Witches. A bit of the plant worn on the person is said to have won the day in court judgements, business matters and in more personal contests of willpower. As a love charm, it is the herb strewn over fire with the incantation:

It's not the herb that I now burn,
But...........'s heart I mean to turn,
May he no peace nor comfort find
Ere he bend to me in soul and mind.

In ancient times it was the custom upon Midsummer Eve (June 20) to build great fires and bid farewell to the Sun as it began its annual retreat. From Summer to Winter Solstice (June 21 to December 21) the daylight hours grow shorter and each day the Sun appears to sink lower in the sky at noon. The coming of Christianity failed to eliminate the age-old fire festival but did manage to alter the date and change the name to celebrate the birthday of their own St. John the Baptist (June 24). That is why today a sacred herb of Witchcraft, Midsummer and the Sun bears the name of a Christian saint.

Hans Christian Andersen

The Money Box

In a nursery where a number of toys lay scattered about, a money-box stood on the top of a very high wardrobe. It was made of clay in the shape of a pig and had been bought of the potter. In the back of the pig was a slit and this slit had been enlarged with a knife, so that dollars, or crown pieces, might slip through; and, indeed there were two in the box, besides a number of pence. The money-pig was stuffed so full that it could no longer rattle, which is the highest state of perfection to which a money-pig can attain. There he stood upon the cupboard, high and lofty, looking down upon everything else in the room. He knew very well that he had enough inside him to buy up all the other toys and this gave him a very good opinion of his own value. The rest thought of this fact also, although they did not express it, for there were so many other things to talk about. A large doll, still handsome, though rather old, for her neck had been mended, lay inside one of the drawers which was partly open. She called out to the others, "Let us have a game at being men and women, that is something worth playing at."

Upon this there was a great uproar; even the engravings, which hung in frames on the wall, turned round in their excitement and showed that they had a wrong side to them, although they had not the least intention to expose themselves in this way, or to object to the game. It was late at night, but as the Moon shone through the windows, they had light at a cheap rate. And as the game was now to begin, all were invited to take part in it, even the children's wagon, which certainly belonged to the coarser playthings.

"Each has its own value," said the wagon; "we cannot all be noblemen; there must be some to do the work."

The money-pig was the only one who received a written invitation. He stood so high that they were afraid he would not accept a verbal message. But in his reply, he said, if he had to take a part, he must enjoy the sport from his own home they were to arrange for him to do so; and so they did. The little toy theatre was therefore put up in such a way that the money-pig could look directly into it. Some wanted to begin with a comedy and afterwards to have a tea party and a discussion for mental improvement, but they commenced with the latter first. The rocking-horse spoke of training and races; the wagon of railways and steam power, for these subjects belonged to each of their professions and it was right they should talk of them. The clock talked politics—"tick, tick"—he professed to know what was the time of day, but

there was a whisper that he did not go correctly. The bamboo cane stood by, looking stiff and proud: he was vain of his brass ferrule and silver top and on the sofa lay two worked cushions, pretty but stupid. When the play at the little theatre began, the rest sat and looked on; they were requested to applaud and stamp, or crack, when they felt gratified with what they saw. But the riding-whip said he never cracked for old people, only for the young who were not yet married. "I crack for everybody," said the cracker.

"Yes and a fine noise you make" thought the audience, as the play went on.

It was not worth much, but it was very well played and all the characters turned their painted sides to the audience, for they were made only to be seen on one side. The acting was wonderful, excepting that sometimes they came out beyond the lamps, because the wires were a little too long. The doll, whose neck had been darned, was so excited that the place in her neck burst and the money-pig declared he must do something for one of the players, as they had all pleased him so much. So he made up his mind to remember one of them in his will, as the one to be buried with him in the family vault, whenever that event should happen. They all enjoyed the comedy so much, that they gave up all thoughts of the tea party and only carried out their idea of intellectual amusement, which they called playing at men and women; and there was nothing wrong about it, for it was only play. All the while, each one thought most of himself, or of what the money-pig could be thinking. His thoughts were on, as he supposed, a very distant time—of making his will and of his burial and of when it might all come to pass. Certainly sooner than he expected—for all at once down he came from the top of the press, fell on the ground and was broken to pieces. Then the pennies hopped and danced about in the most amusing manner. The little ones twirled round like tops and the large ones rolled away as far as they could, especially the one great silver crown piece who had often to go out into the world and now he had his wish as well as all the rest of the money. The pieces of the money-pig were thrown into the dust-bin and the next day there stood a new money-pig on the cupboard, but it had not a farthing in its inside yet and therefore, like the old one, it could not rattle. This was the beginning with him and we will make it the end of our story.

—HANS CHRISTIAN ANDERSEN

Strolling Down Clown Alley

Clowns. Twisted strands of humor and horror combining happiness with the grotesque. With electric orange hair topped by a ridiculously tiny hat, huge shoes, bright, baggy clothes and makeup with exaggerated features, the archetypal clown's purpose is complex and magical. The goal is to establish instant rapport with onlookers and affect a situation. Elements of incongruence and the unexpected come into a play when a clown appears. Balloon work, juggling, acrobatics and amusing magic tricks all set to cheerful calliope music at the circus are how the 'good' professional clowns present themselves.

During the 1960's Bozo the Clown was such an endearing figure. His stunts brought pleasure to millions of viewers on weekly television programs. Patch Adams, M.D. was another beloved clown. For over 40 years Dr. Adams,

in costume, visited hospital patients to bring the healing gift of laughter. Patch told audiences to "speak only of joy in their lives." If there was no joy he would make them laugh by telling them to "lie anyway." *Patch Adams* was a popular movie starring Robin Williams.

In 1963 Ronald McDonald joined McDonald's as an appealing clown spokesman. Ronald charmed children of all ages over fast food meals. The Ronald McDonald House followed in the tradition of Patch Adams as a charity to create a positive environment for the families of children hospitalized for serious illnesses. Emmett Kelly and Red Skelton played endearing hobo or tramp clowns who became media sensations during the 20th Century. Many will recall smiling at Willie and Freddie the Freeloader.

Ancient Laughter

Clowning has its roots in ancient Egypt as far back the 5th dynasty, about 2500 BCE. In China about 300 BCE a famous clown named Yu Sze was a popular court jester. Because he had the ear of the Emperor this clever clown saved thousands of lives. The Emperor wanted to use forced labor to paint the Great Wall white, a task which surely would have sacrificed many. Yu Sze won the hearts of the people by humorously pointing out the absurdity of this project.

Clown-like relics have been incorporated into various ceremonies to invoke sympathetic magic throughout the ages. The addition of comedy to reinforce solemn rites reached Greece and Rome. The rituals of the Hopi Tribe of America's Southwest were also brightened by interlopers wearing humorous masks and costumes. By the Middle Ages, dwarves and jesters, often dressed in belled caps and bright garments, were kept like valued pets in royal courts. Amusing, yet able to answer back to authorities, these characters began to develop into the contemporary clown. Don Rice was an historic clown whose character evolved into Uncle Sam — a caricature for the government, wearing a top hat, whiskers with a star striped suit and trousers in the colors of the Flag. As Uncle Sam, Rice campaigned for President Zachary Taylor and the Presidential Election of 1848 was swayed by a bit of clowning around. Another U.S. President, Richard Nixon, loved clowns so much that he established National Clown Week. It is still observed yearly from August 1-7.

The word clown originally referred to a lout, a bumpkin with poor manners. A loser, a target of ridicule, he or she made others laugh. Think of the class clown. In school the clown tends to be a poor student, annoying yet charismatic and memorable. Perhaps that's because clowns can make us feel better about ourselves. Sometimes.

Painted Joy

There have always been those who secretly mistrust and even fear clowns. During the 1800s Joseph Grimaldi, a stage personality, created his playful and enthusiastic "Joey," a prototype and slang term for the red and white clowns used to this day. In his memoirs Joey Grimaldi admits "I am grim all day, but I make you laugh at night." His personal life was alcoholic, lonely and tragic. Some of his stunts bordered on criminality. Perhaps that's when the trouble slowly began to brew. The pranks, the clowns' elements of caricature and tomfoolery, can have a sinister, even a sadistic side. Coulrophobia, the intense fear of clowns, is on the rise. It affects a large segment of the population spanning all ages. Professional clowns, the good ones, have become very concerned about this trend. Ronald McDonald was recently fired from McDonald's because he began to inspire more fear than joy.

Sinister Smiles

The demand for clowns as entertainers at birthday parties and other events has dissolved. A horror genre of killer clowns seems to be expanding into real life pranks. Perhaps this intensified when Stephen King introduced Pennywise, the murderous clown in his novel followed by two films, titled *IT*. An episode of *The Simpsons* shows Bart cowering in terror as he fears a clown is about to eat him.

Emmett Kelly was tapped to play the role of a homicidal clown in the film *The Fat Man*, but he refused to compromise Willie, his tramp character. Instead Kelly appeared on set as a generic white face clown with tufts of red hair and painted tear drops.

Then there was John Wayne Gacy. Until his arrest for more than 30 murders the serial killer was known around Chicago, masquerading as a respected member of the community and a popular, affable entertainer: Pogo the Clown. In prison Gacy spent his time painting clown portraits.

The 21st Century finds many real life pranksters periodically appearing dressed as clowns. This phenomenon has been observed in almost every State and in numerous countries throughout Europe, in Mexico and Canada. Often brandishing knives or baseball bats as weapons mysterious clowns have been seen wandering along dark streets or at the edges of parks and wooded areas. They dart into view, at a distance usually, then disappear. Many of these characters seem to get a thrill out of terrifying children. When asked they have been heard to say that "the clowns live in a cottage in the woods." Predatory clown sightings seem to come in cycles. Often near Halloween they will peak. While not actually illegal, stalker-clown activities are dangerous, as much for the pranksters as the intended targets. Some clowns have been chased by mobs, attacked and beaten. Recently costume shops have even refused to stock clown outfits, once very popular, fearing that either the would-be clown or victims could be harmed.

Comedic Precepts

Clown Alleys, a term for the cavalcade of dedicated entertainers and the places where they prepare for their acts, are honking the bulb horns in genuine alarm. Clowns of America International, an organization of professional clowns, wants to overcome the bad juju. Abel, "Dimples," the Clown has led the way in promoting *The Eight Clown Commandments* as a step toward restoring the transcendent joy, humor and affection to be offered in the intriguing art and craft of the long-standing clowning tradition.

The Eight Clown Commandments

1. I will keep my acts, performance and behavior in good taste while I am in costume and makeup. I will remember at all times that I have been accepted as a member of the clown club only to provide others, principally children, with clean clown comedy entertainment. I will remember that a good clown entertains others by making fun of himself or herself and not at the expense or embarrassment of others.

2. I will learn to apply my makeup in a professional manner. I will provide my own costume. I will carry out my appearance and assignment for the entertainment of others and not for personal gain or personal publicity when performing for either the International Club or alley events. I will always try to remain anonymous while in makeup and costume as a clown, though there may be circumstances when it is not reasonably possible to do so.

3. I will neither drink alcoholic beverages nor smoke while in makeup or clown costume. Also, I will not drink alcoholic beverages prior to any clown appearances. I will conduct myself as a gentleman/lady, never interfering with other acts, events, spectators or individuals. I will not become involved in or tolerate sexual harassment or discrimination on the basis of race, color, religion, sex, national origin, age, disability or any protected status.

4. I will remove my makeup and change into my street clothes as soon as possible following my appearance, so that I cannot be associated with any incident that may be detrimental to the good name of clowning. I will conduct myself as a gentleman/lady at all times.

5. While on appearance in makeup and costume, I will carry out the directives of the producer or his designated deputies. I will abide by all performance rules without complaint in public.

6. I will do my very best to maintain the best clown standards of makeup, costuming, properties and comedy.

7. I will appear in as many clown shows as I possibly can.

8. I will be committed to providing an atmosphere free of discrimination and harassment for clowns of all ages to share ideas and learn about the art of clowning.

—KOO TEMPLETON

ERIS

A Message From The Newest Planet In Your Horoscope

ASTROLOGY has been practiced around the world in a variety of ways for over five thousand years. Horoscopes, diagrams of the sky mapped by astrologers to interpret messages from above, originally included the luminaries or great lights (the Sun and Moon) and the five visible planets: Mercury, Venus, Mars, Jupiter and Saturn. The fainter but still visible fixed stars were also taken into consideration. The universe, as humanity perceived it, stopped there.

Gradually, as knowledge and technology expanded, an awareness of more planets and their potential influence grew. During the 1700s Uranus was discovered. As telescopes and observation techniques became more sophisticated, Neptune, Pluto, Chiron, the asteroids and a variety of other celestial bodies were discovered. Each new discovery coincided with life on Earth expanding and entering a new phase. Currently our knowledge of the universe is growing at an incredible pace. Space probes and powerful telescopes are steadily revealing amazing facts about how vast and mysterious the familiar planets as well as the new ones observed in deep space really are. As humanity develops the technology to observe new celestial bodies and patterns in the universe, we will be able to more fully understand and respond to them.

An area dubbed the Kuiper Belt has been observed in recent years. It marks the perimeter of our solar system and appears as a doughnut-like formation filled with strange, icy objects. Eris can be found at the edge of the Kuiper Belt. Discovered on January 5, 2005, this new planet orbits our Sun in a vast ellipse. Eris travels completely around the Sun every 560 years and therefore remains in each zodiac sign for a very long time. Eris first entered Aries in 1923 and won't leave that sign until 2044. Nearly everyone alive today will have Eris in Aries in their birth charts. Eris is the largest known body in the solar system not visited by a space craft. It is 27% more massive than Pluto, and, along with Pluto and the asteroid Ceres, has been classified as a dwarf planet. This makes Eris a significant player in the web of energy interpreted in astrological charts. Yet this planet's influence is multigenerational, describing whole cycles of time and groups of people.

Ancient tales of the Greek and Roman gods for whom the planets are named really do illustrate the actual ways the celestial bodies operate. Somehow the scientists and astronomers have always been inspired to correctly name each planet, moon and asteroid upon discovery for the original mythological archetypes whose influences they correlate with in astrology. The role the Greek goddess Eris played in mythology reveals what can be expected with the discovery of this planet. Eris is the Greek goddess of mischief, chaos and strife who delighted in battle and running amok. It was she who tossed the Apple of Discord into the wedding of Peleus and Thetis, starting the Trojan War. An entity of primeval fury who wanders in the infinite darkness, Eris embodies the forces of envy and resentment.

With effort, the influence of Eris can reach a higher level of expression. The goal is to direct the force of this planet in the birth chart into the determination and willpower to generate the extra effort needed to assure triumph. Eris was a sister and companion to Ares/Mars. Astrologically, Eris is increasingly identified as a co-ruler along with Venus over the sign of Libra, the Scales. The balance can tip toward justice or injustice, war or peace. If this rulership over Libra holds true, then Eris' current transit in Aries is oppose the sign of rulership. This places transiting Eris in Aries in its sign of detriment. Between the Spring Equinox of 2018 and the end of winter 2019 Eris moves only from 23 degrees Aries 10 minutes to 23 degrees Aries 22 minutes, a mere fraction of a degree. This places it in the third decanate of Aries, which is co-ruled by Mars and Jupiter. The Sabian Symbol for this degree reads "Blown inward by the wind the curtains of an open window take the shape of a cornucopia." The message here is that outward energies

can be directed inward to facilitate fruition on a subtle, perhaps spiritual level. Also suggested is a yearning for greater riches, to comforts and attaining luxury items. This degree of Aries combined with the Eris transit hints at a desire to make the most of opportunities and a tendency to become more acquisitive.

Distant as it is, this newly introduced member of our solar system family seems quite powerful. Since its discovery unpredictable weather, upsets in the status quo of governments around the world, and general chaos have accelerated. It's important to remember the concept of free will within limits. The stars impel, but don't compel. Here are some thoughts about how to understand and direct this long-term Eris transit. Consider first your Sun sign, then read the entry for your ascendant for deeper insight.

Cardinal Signs
Aries, Cancer, Libra and Capricorn
The Eris transit impacts houses 10, 7, 4 and 1, the angles in your solar chart. Personal appearance, home, partnerships and career aspirations are keynotes. These houses address the present. There is a sense of immediacy.

Fixed Signs
Taurus, Leo, Scorpio and Aquarius
The Eris transit activates houses 12, 9, 6 and 3, the cadent houses in your solar chart. Reverie, education, health and travel can play a role in how it manifests for you. These houses bring reminders of the past. Memories and history come into play.

Mutable Signs
Gemini, Virgo, Sagittarius and Pisces
The Eris transit highlights houses 11, 8, 5 and 2, the succedent houses. Group affiliations, reincarnation and the spirit world, creative expression and financial values are significant factors. These houses relate to latent potentials and the future.

Since Eris has been discovered so recently, studying it offers intriguing opportunities to conduct new research in astrology. For those who would like to pursue this, an accurate ephemeris for Eris can be found at this link:

https://astrology.richardbrown.com/newplanets/eris-eph.shtml

DIKKI-JO MULLEN

Doctor John

The Magic in the Medicine

New Orleans is a city of history and mystery. One of the most famous characters in that true story is Dr. John Montanee. Until recently very little has been known about this legendary figure also known as "Voudoo John" or "John Grisgris." Despite this Dr. John has been an iconic figure for almost two hundred years. He stands as a forefather of New Orleans Voodoo from which much magic has flowed forth. Voodoo in the Crescent City is an ever-evolving spiritual tradition. As our knowledge and access to information about John Montanee grows, so does our power and understanding of his sacred prowess. According to his obituary by Voodoo scholar Lafcadio Hearn in an 1885 *Harper's Weekly*: "no black hierophant now remains capable of manifesting such mystic knowledge or of inspiring such respect as Voudoo John exhibited and compelled."

There is much speculation as to how he became known as Doctor. He is listed as a free person of color in the 1850 census in New Orleans. This document lists his workplace as coffeehouse, which some have theorized could have been used as a synonym for brothel. By the time of the 1860 census, John Montanee's profession is listed as physician, under which the word "quack" is written. Anyone familiar with magic and conjure in the Southern U.S. knows the title Doctor was often conferred on spiritual practitioners who focused on healing. The 1800s in New Orleans was certainly a difficult time for both slaves and free people of color, they would have needed both healing and spiritual services they were otherwise denied. Psychic practitioners like Dr. John stepped up to fill this void.

It's almost impossible to think about Dr. John without thinking of music. It is said the original Dr. John was a drummer for the Voodoo Queen Marie Laveau. Together they held open ceremonies and rituals for all residents of New Orleans regardless of class or color. The music was part of his healing magic and the distant sound of his drums echoes through the city today.

Root Work

Another nickname of John Montanee's was John Racine. Racine means root and there is no doubt that this icon was well versed in the magical use of plants. He practiced creole medicine and used his knowledge of local and readily available herbs to help and heal his community. The following herbs and botanicals can be used in magical baths, gris-gris (herbal mixtures) or just as offerings to honor this powerful spiritual ancestor.

Hi-John the Conqueror Root— The botanical name for this root is *Ipomoea jalapa* and it is a relative of the common morning glory. Hi-John root is one of the most popular herbs in New Orleans Voodoo. People use it for justice, eloquence, money, healing, power, love, gambling and just about everything you can imagine. It can be grated or shaved and used in gris-gris bags or sprinkling powders. Some people just carry it whole.

Lo-John Root—The botanical name for this root is *Alpinia galanga*. It is also known as "little John to chew," which most likely comes from the custom of chewing it in your mouth and then spitting it out as part of a ritual or spell. It is primarily used in workings of justice and equality. Lo-John helps to bring focus, clarity and manifestation to your workings. On the other side of the coin it can be employed for hex breaking and curse removal. Like most of the other herbs on this list it has been in use in the U.S. for over a hundred years and would have been known to herbalists like Dr. John Montanee.

Lavender—This plant is actually many different plants classified botanically under the name *Lavendula*. In New Orleans Voodoo practice it is used very often for love. This could have been brought over from Europe, where ladies of the night were often referred to as "Lavenders" because they were also laundresses who washed their clothes in lavender water. This is documented in Ruth Mazo Karras' *Common Women: Prostitution and Sexuality in Medieval England*.

Ginger—The botanical name for this plant is Zingiber officinale. Ginger is used magically for healing and luck. Either powdered ginger can be used in your offerings or the entire root can be dressed and anointed for a specific purpose. Ginger is said to be ruled by Mars and Aries, so it makes a good choice when trying to access the masculine power of Dr. John.

Cedar—The common name Cedar is used to identify a wide variety of plants going by the botanical classifications of *Juniperus Virginiana, Cedrus Doedara, Cedrus Atlantica, Cedrus Libani* and others. Cedar is used for luck, money, protection spells and potions. Most often the oil is used, but you can also use the bark and leaves in your magic. Some modern practitioners in New Orleans used the shreds as a base for incense, combining it with others herbs and oils to create a powerful blend.

Cypress—Cypress is the common name for a wide variety of plants in the botanical genus *Cupressus*. Cypress is used magically for power, protection, hex breaking and curse removal. Cypress trees are common to New Orleans and the plant is therefore a popular ingredient in both spells and spaces.

Dr. John's ashe, or sacred force, when I have witnessed it, is tribal and transformational. He embraces with healing and heartiness all who approach him with true respect and honor. Magic often functions a lot like medicine and sometimes we all need a good doctor.

—LILITH DORSEY

DOREEN VALIENTE

The Mother of Modern Witchcraft

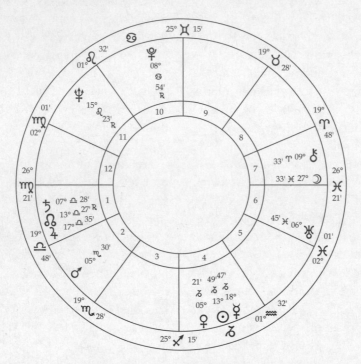

Doreen Valiente's life-long affinity for the Old Ways began with an early childhood spiritual experience as she gazed at the Moon. She began practicing the Occult Arts by the time she was 13 years of age, gleaning a working knowledge of magical practices from reading library books. Her first spell was probably one performed to protect her mother from being harassed at work. Young Doreen's belief in and enthusiasm for the occult was reinforced when that ritual worked.

She was born Doreen Edith Dominy at 10:45 pm on Wednesday, January 4, 1922 at Collier's Wood in Mitcham, Surrey, just South of London, to very conventional and religious parents. It is intriguing to note her Christian baptism never took place because

her mother had an argument with the local vicar. Doreen's Sun, Mercury and Venus form a stellium in her 4th house in Capricorn. In typical Capricorn fashion, she was a serious and thoughtful young person who began planning a career as an artist while still in her teens.

Her Venus is very strongly aspected. It sextiles both Uranus and Mars, opposes Pluto and squares Saturn. This reveals inherent ability that was delayed and thwarted by external factors. With Saturn, the Moon's North Node and Jupiter in Libra, Doreen's natural aptitude for design and color is indicated. This is enhanced by mutual reception between Saturn in Libra and Venus in Capricorn. Uranus in Pisces, Pluto in Cancer and Mars in Scorpio form a grand trine in water signs. This generates great creativity, intuition and sensitivity. Her drawings and other artwork reveal genuine talent. However, her parents Harry and Edith Dominy were concerned about their daughter's interest in magic. To discourage this they sent her away to convent school. Doreen despised school and ran away at age 15. She tried to attend art college, but instead had to accept a job in a factory to support herself. Later she managed to find work as a clerk-typist in a government office. Her 10th house Pluto in Cancer opposes her Capricorn placements and squares her Libra planets. This forms an angular cardinal sign T-square, a pattern which shows challenges and struggles as well as a tendency to take action. Aries is at the open end of the cardinal T-Square, generating assertiveness and a pioneer spirit.

Mars in Scorpio in her 2nd house linked her fortunes to both the military and the sea. During World War II, while working as a translator, she met her first husband, a seaman in 1941. She was just 19. Just five months later she was widowed when he was killed in action in a U-boat attack off the coast of Africa. Gemini rules her mid-heaven, showing versatility and variety in her career, combined with Pluto in the 10th this shows elements of mystery in her public life. During 1942–43 she held several jobs which were probably a cover for intelligence work. At that time Doreen met her second husband, Casimiro Valiente. They married in 1944 and moved to Bournemouth, where they lived with her mother. Casimiro worked as a chef. There is a mutable sign on her 7th house cusp. Her Moon, always an indicator of changes rises on her descendant. This indicates more than one

marriage. Her Chiron in Aries in her 7th house also shows she was able to begin again after overcoming suffering and sacrifice, following her early marriage.

It was at this time that her fascination with Ceremonial Magic and Witchcraft intensified. Doreen had Neptune in Leo in her 11th house, showing an affinity for attracting mystical friends and group associations. She met a friend identified as "Zerki" and commenced practicing Ceremonial Magic with him, using the regalia and tools of art obtained from a member of the Alpha et Omega, a splinter group of the Golden Dawn. At the local library Doreen found Crowley's *Magick in Theory and Practice*, which she read avidly. This inspired her to assume the magical name of "Ameth" and to study Hebrew. Her Part of Fortune in her 3rd house in Sagittarius describes her ability to learn on her own and a love of reading. Spiritualism and Theosophy came into her life during the 1940s and 1950s along with craft-oriented books by Robert Graves, Margaret Murray and Charles Godfrey Leland.

When she read a magazine titled *Witchcraft in Britain* featuring the opening of a center dedicated to Witchcraft on the Isle of Man, she contacted Cecil Williamson, the director. He put her in touch with Edith Woodford-Grimes who in turn introduced her to Gerald Gardner. Doreen felt an immediate connection with Gardner. On the Midsummer's Day Sabbat in 1953 Gardner initiated her into the Bricket Wood Coven. She soon rose to the position of High Priestess.

Doreen's poetic abilities were made available to Gardner as he began adding to the bare bone set of rituals he received during his initiation. Doreen is credited with a number of passages in the Gardnerian ritual book, known as the Book of Shadows. It is believed she wrote several chants which would become important in the future of the Craft—notably "The Witches Rune" and the Full Moon chant beginning "Queen of the Moon and Queen of the Stars…" She was instrumental in the reworking of The Charge of the Goddess—the inspirational piece of liturgy at the core of Wiccan spirituality. Her Virgo ascendant indicates a precise and expressive personality. Doreen grew highly critical of the teachings of Gardner and dedicated her efforts to correcting them, with the goal of protecting the purity of Witchcraft. This angered other Craft practitioners, one of whom described her as "a myopic, stalky nymph." A schism soon developed. Valiente became angered by "St. Gerald" and left to form her own coven. Her memorable personality and assertive qualities are indicated by her 1st house Saturn, Moon Node and Jupiter. She was striking in appearance and always elicited a strong reaction upon acquaintance. As the Jupiter placement hints, she was of above average height. As is common with natal Saturn near the ascendant, she had aquiline features and dark hair.

The strong 4th house showed Doreen's desire not to offend her mother, from whom she kept her practice of Witchcraft a secret. In 1962, after her mother passed away, Doreen became more open about her beliefs. Her first book *Where Witchcraft Lives* was published. Soon she was named President of The Witchcraft Association following Sybil Leek's resignation. Media appearances, followed by the publication of her other important books including *An ABC of Witchcraft*, *Witchcraft for Tomorrow* and *Natural Magic*, further established Doreen's position as an important leader in the Craft. Her second husband died in 1972. He had never been interested in esoteric studies and Doreen claimed the marriage had been unhappy. She became active in politics, promoting a variety of liberal causes. During the 1980's and 1990's Valiente befriended members of the expanding Pagan community, including Starhawk, Stuart and Janet Farrar and Gavin Bone.

When she entered The Summerland on September 8, 1999, ill with diabetes and pancreatic cancer, Doreen bequeathed her estate to her final life partner, John Belham-Payne, entrusting him to do the right thing with her collection. He formed a charitable trust to preserve and protect her legacy. It remains accessible to the millions of seekers whose lives she impacted. She has been called the most influential woman in the world of modern Witchcraft. Posthumously she continues to make history. *The Charge of the Goddess: The Poetry of Doreen Valiente* was published in 2000. In 2009 A Day for Doreen was organized by the Centre for Pagan Studies in Central London. The event attracted a sell-out crowd. Following a public Solstice ritual on June 21, 2013, exactly 60 years after her initiation into Gardnerian Witchcraft, a plaque honoring Doreen Valiente was unveiled at Tyson Power Block, Brighton—her final home.

—DIKKI-JO MULLEN

DOREEN EDITH DOMINY VALIENTE
Born January 4, 1922
at 10:45 pm UT in Mitcham, Surrey, England

Data Table
Tropical Placidus Houses

Sun 13 Capricorn 49—4th house

Moon 27 Pisces 33—7th house—waxing Moon in the crescent phase

Mercury 18 Capricorn 47—4th house

Venus 05 Capricorn 21—4th house

Mars 05 Scorpio 30—2nd house

Jupiter 17 Libra 35—1st house

Saturn 07 Libra 28—1st house

Uranus 06 Pisces 45—6th house

Neptune 15 Leo 23—11th house—retrograde

Pluto 08 Cancer 54—10th house—retrograde

Chiron 09 Aries 33—7th house

N. Moon Node (True Node)—13 Libra 27—1st house

Part of Fortune 10 Sagittarius 04—3rd house

Ascendant (Rising Sign) is 26 Virgo 21

Woman Picking Fruit
Battista Franco

153

Nettles

STINGING NETTLES a perennial native to Europe, Africa, Asia and North America, grows along roadsides and in waste places like empty lots. Though many plants with stinging hairs have the word "nettle" in their English name, unless they belong to the genus Urtica, they're not true nettles.

Relieving the Sting

It is said the pain can be likened to a bee sting.

Doing some research you will discover that if you're stung by nettles, you need only to look around for dock (*Rumex crispus*), often called yellow dock or curly dock, for relief. Your search is usually short—a common folk belief holds that wherever you find nettle, you'll always find dock. In the New World alone, there are more than 20 species of Rumex, some originally from Europe. Bitter dock (*Rumex obtusifolius*), the aforementioned yellow dock and patience dock (*Rumex patientia*) are the most prevalent. Ruled by Jupiter, dock is a member of the Buckwheat family.

To stop the nettle's sting, wad up a handful of dock leaves in a tight ball, crushing as hard as you can and rub the resulting juice on the affected area. Medicinal herbals will tell you that's all you need do, but as far back as the 14th century, folklore held that you also needed to recite a charm over and over while you rubbed.

Most versions of the charms direct the nettle sting to come out as the dock goes in. Here are two examples.

Nettle out, dock in,
Dock remove the nettle sting.

Nettle, nettle, come out
Dock, dock, go in

However, one version from Clun, a small town in south Shropshire, England, doesn't follow that formula:

Dock, dock, shall have a smock,
Nettle shall have ne'er a one.

Surprisingly, there are accounts of people *wanting* to be stung. As far back as ancient Egypt and Greece, sufferers would flog themselves with nettle bundles for relief from gout and rheumatism.

Magickal Properties

Its stinging properties place it under the rulership of Mars. It confers strength against fear and can be used to bind a spell. Carry it to prevent being struck by lightning.

Nettle was one of the nine herbs required for the 10th-century rite called the "Nine Herbs Charm" which was used to treat poisoning and infection. *The Lacnunga Manuscript* recorded the technique and words to be sung during its preparation.

Textile Strength

Despite its nasty sting, nettles have been important in textile crafts. It was formerly grown in Scotland for its fibers, which were used to make a cloth called nettle-linen. Stronger than regular linen, its strength increase when wet. At one time, nettle fiber was used to make rope and paper, while natural dye enthusiasts use nettle leaves to make green dye.

Culinary Tastes

If that isn't already enough to turn our hearts softer toward the cruel plant, if harvested and prepared properly, it's a delicious food. Only spring nettles in their first growth that have not yet flowered and are less than a foot high are edible. Use thick gloves to harvest them and remove the leaves from the stem. You must boil or otherwise heat them to remove the sting.

Various recipes exist. The simplest is serving cooked young tops with butter as you would serve spinach. Simmer it with onion and potatoes for a delicious soup. Add sorrel and seasonings at the end and puree. With phyllo pastry, feta cheese, parsley and mint, you can make Sigara Borek, a classic snack from Turkey. With a little water, sugar and time, you can even make nettle beer.

—MORVEN WESTFIELD

Moon Cycles

A New Moon rises with the Sun,
Her waxing half at midday shows,
The Full Moon climbs at sunset hour,
And waning half the midnight knows.

NEW	2019	FULL	NEW	2020	FULL
January 5		January 21			January 10
February 4		February 19	January 24		February 9
March 6		March 20	February 23		March 9
April 5		April 19	March 24		April 7
May 4		May 18	April 22		May 7
June 3		June 17	May 22		June 5
July 2, 31**		July 16	June 21		July 5
August 30		August 15	July 20		August 3
September 28		September 14	August 18		September 2
October 27		October 13	September 17		October 1
November 26		November 12	October 16		October 31*
December 26		December 12	November 15		November 30
			December 14		December 29

* Blue Moon on October 31, 2020.

** July 31 A rare second New Moon in the same month is called a Black Moon. Occurring on July 31, 2019, it is sacred to the fey ones.

Life takes on added dimension when you match your activities to the waxing and waning of the Moon. Observe the sequence of her phases to learn the wisdom of constant change within complete certainty.

Dates are for Eastern Standard and Daylight Time.

presage

by Dikki-Jo Mullen

ARIES, 2018–PISCES, 2019

The Wheel of Time resets to start at the Vernal Equinox, marking a new zodiacal cycle. Springtime ushers in a longing for new life. As the last shadows of the dull winter are gradually refreshed by outbursts of color, humanity looks toward hope and growth. The wisdom of the heavens, through astrology, provides a map offering guidance and understanding.

The spirituality sections of each Presage forecast this year suggest a rune for the individual birth signs. The runes are sacred symbols, released from the Well of Urd to Odin, the Norse god of knowledge and poetry, after he proved himself worthy by fasting and hanging upside down from Yggdrasil, the World Tree, in self-sacrifice for nine days.

The planet Uranus, ruler of the unexpected and of sudden changes, begins a new seven-year cycle as it crosses the Aries-Taurus cusp. Ecology and the economy are topics which are due for a shake-up. From mid-May through mid-November Mars makes a long passage through Aquarius and the Capricorn cusp, accenting finances, politics and human rights issues. There are five eclipses, two total and three partial, this year to interject surprising shifts in the status quo. Two of the eclipses are in Leo, and one each will be in Cancer, Aquarius and Capricorn.

Begin by reading the forecast for your familiar birth sign for an overview of what this dynamic year will mean to you. Then consider your ascendant, or rising sign, for insight into your surroundings and your natal Moon sign to learn about your emotional needs and responses. Those born on the day of a sign change are different. Both forecasts blend into their lives in various ways. Read about all of this and more in Presage.

ASTROLOGICAL KEYS

Signs of the Zodiac
Channels of Expression

ARIES: fiery, pioneering, competitive
TAURUS: earthy, stable, practical
GEMINI: dual, lively, versatile
CANCER: protective, traditional
LEO: dramatic, flamboyant, warm
VIRGO: conscientious, analytical
LIBRA: refined, fair, sociable
SCORPIO: intense, secretive, ambitious
SAGITTARIUS: friendly, expansive
CAPRICORN: cautious, materialistic
AQUARIUS: inquisitive, unpredictable
PISCES: responsive, dependent, fanciful

Elements

FIRE: Aries, Leo, Sagittarius
EARTH: Taurus, Virgo, Capricorn
AIR: Gemini, Libra, Aquarius
WATER: Cancer, Scorpio, Pisces

Qualities

CARDINAL	FIXED	MUTABLE
Aries	Taurus	Gemini
Cancer	Leo	Virgo
Libra	Scorpio	Sagittarius
Capricorn	Aquarius	Pisces

CARDINAL signs mark the beginning of each new season — active.
FIXED signs represent the season at its height — steadfast.
MUTABLE signs herald a change of season — variable.

Celestial Bodies
Generating Energy of the Cosmos

Sun: birth sign, ego, identity
Moon: emotions, memories, personality
Mercury: communication, intellect, skills
Venus: love, pleasures, the fine arts
Mars: energy, challenges, sports
Jupiter: expansion, religion, happiness
Saturn: responsibility, maturity, realities
Uranus: originality, science, progress
Neptune: dreams, illusions, inspiration
Pluto: rebirth, renewal, resources

Glossary of Aspects

Conjunction: two planets within the same sign or less than 10 degrees apart, favorable or unfavorable according to the nature of the planets.

Sextile: a pleasant, harmonious aspect occurring when two planets are two signs or 60 degrees apart.

Square: a major negative effect resulting when planets are three signs from one another or 90 degrees apart.

Trine: planets four signs or 120 degrees apart, forming a positive and favorable influence.

Quincunx: planets are 150 degrees or about 5 signs apart. The hand of fate is at work and unique challenges can develop. Sometimes a karmic situation emerges.

Opposition: a six-sign or 180° separation of planets generating positive or negative forces depending on the planets involved.

The Houses — *Twelve Areas of Life*

1st house: appearance, image, identity
2nd house: money, possessions, tools
3rd house: communications, siblings
4th house: family, domesticity, security
5th house: romance, creativity, children
6th house: daily routine, service, health

7th house: marriage, partnerships, union
8th house: passion, death, rebirth, soul
9th house: travel, philosophy, education
10th house: fame, achievement, mastery
11th house: goals, friends, high hopes
12th house: sacrifice, solitude, privacy

Eclipses

Elements of surprise, odd weather patterns, change and growth are linked to eclipses. Those with a birthday within three days of an eclipse can expect some shifts in the status quo. There are five eclipses this year; three are partial and two are total.

July 12, 2018 New Moon partial solar eclipse in Cancer, north node

July 27, 2018 Full Moon total lunar eclipse in Aquarius, south node

August 11, 2018 New Moon partial solar eclipse in Leo, north node

January 5, 2019 New Moon partial solar eclipse in Capricorn, south node

January 21, 2019 Full Moon total lunar eclipse in Leo, north node

A total eclipse is more influential than a partial. The eclipses conjunct the Moon's north node are thought to be more favorable than those conjunct the south node.

Retrograde Planetary Motion

Retrogrades promise a change of pace, different paths and perspectives.

Mercury Retrograde

Impacts technology, travel and communication. Those who have been out of touch return. Revise, review and tread familiar paths. Affected: Gemini and Virgo.

Mar. 22, 2018–Apr. 15, 2018
in Aries
July 26, 2018–Aug. 19, 2018
in Leo
Nov. 16, 2018–Dec. 6, 2018 in Scorpio and Sagittarius Mar. 5, 2019–Mar. 28, 2019
in Pisces

Venus Retrograde

Influences art, finances and love. Affected: Taurus and Libra.

Oct. 5, 2018–Nov. 16, 2018
in Scorpio and Libra

Mars Retrograde

The military, sports and heavy industry are impacted. Affected: Aries and Scorpio.

June 26, 2018–Aug. 27, 2018
in Aquarius and Capricorn

Jupiter Retrograde

Large animals, learning and religion are impacted. Affected: Sagittarius and Pisces.

Mar. 8, 2018–July 10, 2018 in Scorpio

Saturn Retrograde

Elderly people, the disadvantaged, employment and natural resources are linked to Saturn. Affected: Capricorn and Aquarius.

Apr. 17, 2018–Sept. 6, 2018
in Capricorn

Uranus Retrograde

Inventions, science, electronics, revolutionaries and extreme weather relate to Uranus retrograde. Affected: Aquarius.

Aug. 7, 2018–Jan. 6, 2019
in Aries and Taurus

Neptune Retrograde

Water, marine animals, chemicals, spiritual forces and psychic phenomena are impacted by this retrograde. Affected: Pisces.

June 18, 2018–Nov. 24, 2018
in Pisces

Pluto Retrograde

Ecology, espionage, birth and death rates, nuclear power and mysteries relate to Pluto retrograde. Scorpio is affected.

Apr. 22, 2018–Sept. 30, 2018
in Capricorn

ARIES
March 20–April 19

Spring 2018–Spring 2019 for those
born under the sign of the Ram

You are a human dynamo—warm, confident and a natural leader. Make it a habit to add a dash of patience and perseverance, complete all that you start, and the world is yours. Ruled by Mars, you have a competitive streak and thrive on sports, games and physical activity.

The early days of spring are joyful. Musical and artistic Venus brightens your birth sign from the Vernal Equinox through March 31. When Mercury conjoins your Sun from April through May 13, conversations and travel provide catalysts for new ideas and problem-solving. From the end of May through the Summer Solstice the focus shifts to planetary transits affecting your 4th house. Thoughts turn toward your heritage, family life and real estate as the Solstice nears. Dedicate the longest day of the year to a house blessing.

On June 26 an eight-week Mars retrograde cycle commences during which you will revise priorities. The Aquarius lunar eclipse on July 27 augurs an abrupt shift regarding your social circle and personal wishes. By Lammastide your outlook will be changing. The first half of August emphasizes your 5th house of pleasure. Share a favorite hobby or plan a vacation with loved ones.

From August 14 through mid-September Mars joins Saturn in your 10th house. Both of these celestial heavyweights square your Sun, creating a pressure cooker regarding your career. Seek ways to make your work environment more nurturing. Much can be accomplished. There can be a bit of notoriety coming your way before the Autumnal Equinox. September 23–October 10 Mercury impacts your 7th house of partnerships. Take time to listen carefully. Someone has needs and ideas to discuss. An issue emerges. Be understanding and adaptable. The New Moon on October 8 unveils the specifics.

During October transits of Venus, Mercury, Jupiter and the Sun move into your 8th house. You might be inspired to try some paranormal research. Near Halloween a deepening connection with loved ones who have passed away can be felt. Honor them with an ancestor altar and find comfort in cherished memories. In November retrograde Venus highlights your 7th house of relationships while opposing Uranus in your 1st house. A legal matter takes a turn for the better. You may be amazed by a talented associate at the end of the month. December accents the importance of animal companions as well as an appreciation for different spiritual philosophies. Sagittarius transits, including Jupiter, the Sun and Mercury highlight your 9th house. A sophisticated friend shares anecdotes which inspire, amuse and enlighten you.

During December Mars, your ruler, floats with Neptune in Pisces into your 12th house. A quiet mood intensifies as the month ends. You will relish rest and reverie. Try dream interpretation near the Winter Solstice. Charitable projects bring peace and satisfaction during the winter holidays. As January begins there is renewed energy and enthusiasm. Mars enters Aries where it conjoins your Sun. You'll be drawn to expend extra effort and make some major changes in the status quo. Career ambitions can be a part of this. On January 6 Mercury activates your sector of fame and fortune. You'll assume a higher profile during the first three weeks of the new year.

On January 21 the Full Moon in Leo completes a grand trine with transits in the other fire signs. Late January through mid-February is happy and upbeat. There is more time to follow your heart. An avocation or a close relationship is a part of this. The last half of February brings a focus on security, as Mars enters your 2nd house of finances. You'll strive to enhance your earning power and acquire desired possessions. Mercury, the Sun and Neptune create a subtle influence in your 12th house during March. Some topics you will want to keep close to your heart. Others might comment on how you seem rather complex or even mysterious. Merely smile and reveal little. The New Moon on March 6 highlights this focus. As the winter ends, appreciate the power inherent in guarding secrets.

HEALTH
July 11–August 6 Venus transits your health sector. Heed constructive suggestions others offer about wholesome foods and lifestyle. Be careful not to get overwhelmed by work or strenuous exercise while Mars is retrograde from late June through late August.

LOVE
The eclipses on August 11 and January 21 both fall your 5th house of romance, promising a year of sparkle and renewed zest in love. Either a present relationship will deepen to a new level of intimacy or a special someone will enter your life unexpectedly. Sharing a favorite leisure time pursuit sets the scene for romance.

SPIRITUALITY
Jupiter transits your 8th house until early November. This deepens your awareness of reincarnation, the afterlife and connections with the spiritual realm. The Full Moon on April 29 activates this influence. Spiritual workings near Beltane can be especially meaningful. *Mannaz*, the rune which links to Aries, honors the higher self. It can be helpful in strengthening spirituality and self acceptance.

FINANCE
May 16–November 6 Uranus touches the cusp of your 2nd house of finances. Be alert to any new economic trends and changes in your source of income which are manifesting. Resist being pressured by others; trust your instincts. Your financial situation should brighten after November 9 when Jupiter begins a favorable year-long aspect to your Sun.

TAURUS
April 20–May 20
Spring 2018–Spring 2019 for those
born under the sign of the Bull

Your innate tenacity carries you toward successful manifestation regarding everything from nurturing a relationship to reaching career goals. Taurus resonates with the Earth. You have a knack for gardening, camping and ecology. You also appreciate sound. Frequently Taureans are gifted musicians.

Spring begins with Mars and Saturn accenting your 9th house. Plans for travel and enrolling in higher education can be in the works at the Vernal Equinox. Philosophical topics appeal; you'll be in the mood to explore deeper spiritual truths. April 1–23 brings a strong Venus transit. Your beauty and charm impress others favorably. Creative projects and business matters flourish. The Full Moon on April 29 accents partnerships and legalities. By May Day resolutions are reached. Through May 13 Mercury impacts your 12th house. Your privacy will be important. Honor the power inherent in secrecy. Meditation provides a catalyst for retrieving a past life memory and intuitive insights. The New Moon on May 15 generates a deeper self-understanding. The remainder of May is highly competitive. Mars begins a transit through your sector of fame and fortune. Your motivation and ambitions are expanding. During the first half of June, Mercury highlights conversations concerning security issues and earning powers.

By the Summer Solstice Venus enters your 4th house where it remains through July 9. You'll feel inclined to beautify your home, perhaps redecorating or even purchasing an improved residence. Loving concern for family members prevails. In mid-July, Jupiter turns direct in your 7th house. A close partnership deepens and legal matters resolve in your favor. From Lammastide through August 5, Venus favorably aspects your Sun. Summer vacation brings happiness and strengthens a love connection. Uranus in Taurus and Saturn in Capricorn are favorable from mid-August through mid-September. This augurs sudden opportunities to establish greater security and acquire desired possessions. Your hard work will be noticed and appreciated by colleagues. September 7–22 finds Mercury moving rapidly through Virgo, your sister earth sign. Travel can be especially productive during the weeks before the Autumnal Equinox. You are alert and learn a lot.

Autumn begins with a powerful Mars square to your Sun. Tension builds challenges among associates. Dedicate a seasonal ritual to peace and goodwill. It would be wise to diffuse controversy with humor throughout October. At Halloween important transits including Venus and Jupiter oppose your Sun. Cooperate with others regarding which celebrations and events to attend.

By November 16, Mars changes signs. Support and encouragement build. Camaraderie warms your heart and uplifts your spirit. Retrograde Mercury affects your 7th and 8th houses from late November through December 7. Don't repeat patterns that haven't boded well in the past involving shared finances, investments or insurance. An outstanding financial concern should be resolved favorably in December. The Winter Solstice favors rituals connected to truth seeking and serenity. Honor the winter holidays with a gathering of like-minded associates. Early winter finds Jupiter and Neptune in a stressful pattern. Balance paranormal experiences with some grounding and practicality. Verify rumors before taking action.

In January, Mercury conjoins Pluto and the Sun in your 9th house. Faith helps you move forward. Synchronicities offer guidance. Business travel is favorable during January. At Candlemas purify your surroundings with sacred smoke and blessed water. Release memories and habits linked to any long-standing resentments. From mid-February through the end of winter, friends provide information as well as a sounding board. Mercury moves through your 11th house in conjunction with Neptune, bringing valuable insights. New ideas offer a fresh perspective at the New Moon on March 6. Mars transits your Sun as winter draws to a close, providing a burst of energy and confidence. Workloads lighten and you win debates in late March.

HEALTH
The Full Moon in your health sector on April 1 ushers in a four-week cycle of awareness concerning your body image and diet. Formulate a health and fitness plan then to assure wellness throughout the year. Retrograde Venus affects your health October 5–November 16. Resist tempting, high calorie foods or a sedentary lifestyle to overcome health challenges then.

LOVE
July 10–August 5 finds Venus in your 5th house of love. A cherished relationship deepens. Share memorable moments with ones dear to your heart. Offer tokens of your affection and gratitude at Lammastide. The eclipse on August 11 reminds you of how family dynamics are shifting. Allow loved ones to grow and express themselves as summer draws to a close.

SPIRITUALITY
Near your birthday this year, Uranus touches the cusp of Taurus where it remains until retrograding back into Aries in early November. This foreshadows the start of a rare and significant transit which unfolds over the next seven years or so. Major changes in perspective are on the horizon. The deeper messages in your horoscope can serve as a guide; consider esoteric astrology. The Taurus rune, *Feoh*, which means "possessions," can help you fulfill your needs and enhance spiritual strength.

FINANCE
From the Vernal Equinox through early November, Jupiter opposes your Sun. Others will influence your finances. Don't be generous to the point that your own resources are depleted. Let your own better judgment make the final call when others offer suggestions about finances. During April and February, positive earth sign transits favor monetary improvement.

GEMINI
May 21 – June 20
Spring 2018 – Spring 2019 for those
born under the sign of the Twins

Quick-witted with the gift of gab, Gemini is a multi-faceted enigma. Forever changeable, impulsive and charming, you effortlessly adapt to circumstances. With an ability to grasp situations at a glance, you embrace new projects while others are still puzzling about what happened. Still, to fulfill your potential, it's essential for you to concentrate and follow through with what you have begun. Remember that the true value of an action relies upon completion.

From spring's earliest days until April 15, Mercury, your ruler, is retrograde in your 11th house. Expect to reconnect with longtime friends and revisit past interests. Following the New Moon on April 15, an abrupt shift occurs. Loose ends are tied up, and you're ready to move forward. April 25 – May 19 Venus dances through your birth sign. Your charisma is in top form; business and personal relationships are favored. On May Day, plan a gathering and decorate with seasonal flowers and a maypole. Late May through mid-June you'll be ready to explore new ideas as Mercury conjoins your Sun. Travel plans can brighten your birthday. You might be called upon to do some public speaking by the Summer Solstice.

At the end of June, Mars turns retrograde, affecting your 8th and 9th houses. This encourages you to reflect upon your spiritual beliefs. Religion and philosophy can become topics of lively debate during the summer days. Books read during this time can be especially informative and influential. The eclipse on July 27 in Aquarius highlights the specifics. At Lammastide, reflect upon the true meaning of this early harvest celebration, perhaps writing a ritual or poem to honor the occasion. By August 7 Venus enters your sister air sign of Libra where it brightens your 5th house until September 8. Creative projects and hobbies can be fulfilling. Love connections will blossom too. Saturn turns direct in your 8th house in early September. This favors research of any kind, including past life regression and connecting with spiritual dimensions as the Autumn Equinox approaches. An old letter or other message from someone associated with your past surfaces to put a new slant on a sensitive situation.

During October several planetary transits move into your health sector. You will be aware of the mind-body connection, how outlook and attitude can impact wellness. Keep exercise schedules moderate but evenly paced. Extremes of all kinds should be avoided and by Halloween you'll experience renewed vitality. Throughout November, Mercury will activate your 7th house and oppose your Sun. Listen when others express opposing viewpoints. Success is achieved through negotiation and compromise. Near the Gemini Full Moon on November 23, you will have a clear sense of direction.

December emphasizes several contradictory transits in the mutable signs. These aspect your Sun, impacting close associations and loyalties as well as career aspirations. Effort and hard work will assure rewards. The pressures dissipate near the Winter Solstice. A new direction begins to take shape during the dark and quiet days of early winter. Heed messages and symbols which arrive in meditation or remembered dreams. As January begins, Mars enters your 11th house where it favorably aspects your Sun until mid-February. This provides a boost in mental energy. You can learn much through following media coverage or engaging in brainstorming sessions. The eclipses on January 5 and 21 highlight how investment strategies can be tweaked to offer a better financial return. Neighbors become more influential in your life, perhaps providing valuable insights. At Candlemas dedicate white candles to purify bittersweet memories and complex relationships.

February 3–March 1, Venus joins Pluto in your 8th house. Inherited or invested funds add to your security. A payment arrives relieving any anxiety regarding finances. In March, Uranus joins Mars in your 12th house. Charitable work, performing quiet good deeds, will provide satisfaction and inner peace. Winter's final days bring an appreciation for animal companions and places of natural beauty.

HEALTH

From March until November 7, benevolent Jupiter blesses your health sector. Focus on maintaining a wholesome lifestyle and attend to health care then. This will set the stage to assure wellness during the long-range future. Since this transit occurs in a water sign include plenty of fresh water, juices and herbal teas each day to cleanse your system. Examine hereditary factors for further insights concerning health needs.

LOVE

Venus, ruler of your 5th house of love, is favorable during the first three weeks of May and again in March. Someone you care for may draw nearer then. Preserve the status quo regarding love while Venus is retrograde October 5– November 16; otherwise there could be regrets. Heed a sense of déjà vu regarding love near Halloween.

SPIRTUALITY

Your 9th house of spirituality is affected by the eclipse on July 27. Evolving spiritual awakening emerges near that time. This could involve an invitation to attend a different kind of circle or other novel metaphysical gathering with a friend. The rune *Ansuz*, meaning "signal or flag," relates to Mercury, your ruler. It brings valuable insights concerning the power of language and factual information.

FINANCE

The July 12 solar eclipse shakes up your 2nd house of finances. This might point to a different source of income or developing new, salable skills near that time. Be aware of new trends in your field this year. Perform a prosperity ritual at the Summer Solstice. Consider how others are affecting your money. Don't be pressured into acting on risky financial advice and all will be well.

CANCER
June 21 – July 22
Spring 2018 – Spring 2019 for those
born under the sign of the Crab

Thoughtful and patient, you are generous with your resources and time. Affectionate and caring yet reserved, you are sensitive to nuance and have excellent intuition. It's important for Moon Children to realize when it's time to release old regrets and the past in order to completely relish what the present and future have to offer. The Crab holds on to treasures and resources. Usually this translates into a flair for excellent management of finances and wise business decisions.

At the Vernal Equinox the Sun joins Venus, Mercury and Uranus in your 10th house. Thoughts and creative efforts are focused on career goals. There can be innovative options available. Finalize important changes after Mercury completes its retrograde on April 15. Throughout April until May 16, Mars adds fire to your 7th house of partnerships. Others offer suggestions which impact you. There can be some conflicts to resolve and compromises to make. Devote May Eve observances to seeking stress release. Tender-hearted Venus comes to the rescue from late May through June 14 with a transit through your birth sign. Relationships become more

harmonious, and the healing power of love is in evidence. Experiment with crafts and other creative projects during late spring.

A sentimental journey near the Summer Solstice is likely as Mercury highlights your first house then. Travel over water or visit historical sites. Your birthday ushers in a year of surprises, as there will be an eclipse in Cancer on July 12. If you feel jolted out of your comfort zone, keep a sense of humor and be receptive to changes. Your 2nd and 8th houses are highlighted throughout late July and August. Thoughts and conversations will revolve around financial security. An investment, inheritance or the earnings of a partner can augment your personal resources. Thoughtful monetary planning means abundance in your bank account by Lammas.

September finds Saturn completing a retrograde while making a favorable aspect to Uranus. This can release you from an obligation and generate introductions to new people. Consider becoming more active in an organization as the Autumnal Equinox approaches. Community and political concerns can be a part of this. October finds Venus turning retrograde in your love sector. Enjoy the company if an old flame rekindles, but be aware that history might repeat itself for good or ill. Keep the romantic mood light and friendly.

A nostalgic mood arrives with Halloween. Enjoy vintage decorations and costumes as well as greeting cards or photos from years past. Throughout November, Venus impacts your 4th house of home and family life. You will appreciate your home; it becomes your refuge. You might redecorate and plan a home-cooked meal to share.

In December, Mars joins Neptune in Pisces in your 9th house of higher learning and philosophy. You'd enjoy spiritual studies or a trip to celebrate the Winter Solstice in an inspirational location. December 13–January 5, Mercury joins Jupiter in your 6th house. Health takes a turn for the better. Animal companions are nurturing and appreciative. A new pet could find a place in your heart and hearth. Associates are unpredictable in January, as a stir is created by an eclipse in your relationship sector at the beginning of the month. Take care of yourself first and maintain a live-and-let-live attitude toward others. Resist the temptation to cling.

As Candlemas nears, your 8th house is highlighted. A mystery is solved, and there can be messages of comfort received from the spirit world. The accomplishments of a friend delight you during the last half of February when Mars enters your 11th house. Offer deserved compliments and encouragement. March finds your goals and interests in flux. Uranus is changing signs and moves into an aspect to your Sun. You will feel restless and consider new directions as winter wanes. The New Moon on March 6 brings insights. A dream or time spent in contemplative meditation can help you make choices.

HEALTH
During the spring and summer months water sign transits indicate that time spent near the water can facilitate well-being. Jupiter, the most benevolent of planets, will enter your health sector on November 8 for a year-long passage. This promises, wonderful opportunities for overcoming any health challenges. Explore home remedies. They might be very helpful.

LOVE
Saturn and Pluto are affecting your 7th house of partnership and commitment throughout the year. A loved one can be in need of care and encouragement. Heartfelt loyalties involve serious dedication now. Venus transits during both June and December promise happy romantic interludes.

SPIRITUALITY
The eclipse in your birth sign on July 12 awakens a sense of spiritual destiny. Honor the Full Moon in Cancer near the Winter Solstice on December 22. This lunation ushers in profound spiritual connections. The rune of protection, *Algiz*, which translates to "elk and rushes," corresponds to Cancer. It establishes boundaries and stabilizes emotional responses.

FINANCE
June 29–September 5 various celestial transit patterns impact your 2nd house, the money sector. Take time to study financial trends and examine options. Keep a record of expenses and monetary transactions. Information gathered during this time can be of great value in lucrative financial planning.

LEO
July 23–August 22
Spring 2018–Spring 2019 for those
born under the sign of the Lion

Magnetic, dramatic and with a natural warmth, Leos are born leaders. You are affectionate and very loyal with intense opinions about almost everything. Creative and charming, you have a natural dignity which attracts quality. Leo retains a spirit of exuberance. You have a special ability to connect with and inspire young people.

The early days of spring usher in an urge to explore. The Sun joins Venus, Mercury and Uranus to transit your 9th house. New philosophical concepts and distant horizons beckon. As April begins, Venus brightens your career sector. Business and pleasure combine gracefully, and friends promote your best interests through May Eve. Focus on important details and attend to the needs of animal companions during the first half of May while Mars completes a transit through your 6th house. Uranus touches your midheaven on May 15, foreshadowing major career turning points. These will unfold during the long-range future. Situations arise, perhaps involving a sudden offer or desire to initiate change. This can skew your professional goals into a new direction as June begins.

By mid-June Venus is in Leo moving toward a conjunction with your Sun. The Summer Solstice is social. Host a gathering to honor the shortest of nights. The good times roll on through July 10. The July 12 eclipse in your 12th house abruptly shifts priorities. A yearning for peace and privacy develops. You might either want to be alone or in the company of only your nearest and dearest as Lammas approaches. During late July through August 13, retrograde Mars opposes your Sun. Competitive situations are accented. Near your birthday a dynamic associate offers suggestions and presents some ambitious plans. Keep a perspective about how all of this is influencing you. Don't be swept along by peer pressure and all will be well.

Wonderful travel and study opportunities expand your horizons and pique your interest during August and early September when Mercury affects your 1st house. The focus shifts to your financial sector by September 7. Discussions accent money management, security and earning potential during remainder of September. Decorate your altar with fall colors and prosperity symbols. Offer thanks for an abundant early harvest season at the Autumnal Equinox. During October, Venus goes retrograde in your sector of home and family life. Be aware of repeating patterns regarding living arrangements. Look to the past if you would know the future. There are opportunities to address domestic needs. By Halloween you could use a break from home and hearth. Visit a sacred place of natural beauty or historic significance to honor the Sabbat.

Jupiter joins Mercury in your 5th house during November. Younger people have much to share. A recreational activity captivates you. Life is filled with delight and purpose as December begins. The New Moon on December 7 reveals the specifics. Decorating your residence for holiday festivities brings you joy during December because Venus brightens your 4th house. This benevolent trend extends until January 6. A real estate transaction or remodeling project can conclude favorably. At the Winter Solstice, offer a blessing for your home. January brings a lunar eclipse in your birth sign, promising surprises. Accept this; allow old doors to close so new ones can open. The second and third weeks of January favor focusing on health and fitness goals. Analyze how you can make your daily environment and schedule more comfortable and wholesome.

By Imbolc a partner will wish to talk. Listen respectfully to the perspectives of another during February to assure cooperation and success in either the business or personal realm. A competitive mood develops during February. Employ strategy and good sportsmanship to win respect and carry you forward as the month ends. March has a mysterious quality. Several transits gather in your 8th house while forming a quincunx aspect to your Sun. Fate plays a role in events. Heed nuances and synchronicities near the March 6 New Moon. Winter's last days bring many memories to the surface. These can involve past life recollections or messages from spirit guides.

HEALTH

Saturn and Pluto transit your 6th house of health. The Capricorn eclipse on January 5 also impacts well-being. Attune to healthy habits and seek prompt advice for any conditions which arise. Patience and consistency are the keys to good health now. Massaging the lower limbs and attending to cardio exercise should enhance wellness.

LOVE

June 14 through July 9 finds Venus, the celestial love goddess, in Leo. That cycle is very auspicious for romantic bliss. Plan a romantic walk at sunset with one whom you would woo. Jupiter, the most fortunate of planets, enters your 5th house of love on November 8. This is quite promising for developing love connections during the late autumn and winter.

SPIRITUALITY

There are two eclipses in Leo, your 1st house, this year: one on August 11 at the New Moon and one on January 21 at the Full Moon. Events near those dates will awaken spirituality. *Sowelu* is the rune identified with the Sun, your ruler. It relates to vitality, personal power and a sense of direction and success.

FINANCE

Mercury rules your 2nd house of finances. Retrograde Mercury cycles reveal how patterns repeat, for good or not, regarding money matters. Studying and discussing finances can be helpful. You can profit from business travel too. Late July through early September favors financial gain.

VIRGO

August 23–September 22
Spring 2018–Spring 2019 for those
born under the sign of the Virgin

Virgos have a flair for problem-solving. Your dedication to detail, analytical mind and superior communication skills will propel you toward success. Travel, teaching, sales and health care are rewarding career choices. Others can misinterpret your constructive, well-intended observations as being too critical at times. Balance faultfinding by interspersing some positive, encouraging comments. Practical and conventional, you do tend to be a worrier. Planning for the future while using resources and time wisely will assure peace of mind.

As the Vernal Equinox dawns Mercury, your ruler, is poised to turn retrograde in your 8th house. Some old financial obligations or choices about management of resources can require attention. By mid-April decisions will be finalized and you'll feel more relaxed. Venus dances through Taurus, your sister earth sign, from mid to late April. The beauty of the outdoors evokes a spiritual feeling and provides a pleasant backdrop for social situations. A journey would be enjoyable. By late April a businesslike attitude prevails. Mars, Saturn and Pluto aspect your Sun, combining creative ideas with a serious intent. You can accomplish a lot with little effort during the first half of May. From mid-

May through the Summer Solstice transits shift the accent to your 11th house. Friends provide inspiration concerning long-term goals which can accent political issues or involvement in community life.

On June 26 Mars turns retrograde in Aquarius, impacting your health and service sector for the next eight weeks. You can find new ways to effectively diagnose and treat any ongoing health issues. At the same time, the summer months find you focused on improvements in the daily work environment. A significant relationship with a beloved animal companion deepens June–August. By Lammastide you can experience a genuine psychic connection to a special pet. A new animal might join your household during August.

The New Moon in Virgo on September 9 activates a grand trine in the earth signs. This points to a productive cycle. Your responsibilities and workload lighten around your birthday. A visit to an organic garden or other outdoor activities would be enjoyable near the Autumn Equinox. September 23–October 10 Mercury dashes through your 2nd house of money. Be on the alert. Lucrative opportunities appear then. During the remainder of October Jupiter moves toward the late degrees of Scorpio, accenting your 3rd house. You would enjoy films and poems or literature with a gothic, past life or mystical accent. Traditional party games would create a festive mood and evoke happy memories on Halloween.

November finds Mercury and Jupiter transiting your 4th house. New possibilities for growth and expansion highlight your living arrangements then. Real estate transactions or a home improvement project could be on the horizon. Healing a past disappointment and improving lines of communication with family members can deepen your happiness as the winter holiday season begins. Mars joins Neptune to oppose your Sun from late November through December. Others can surprise you by being more assertive than usual. Examine their deeper motives and ask questions to facilitate understanding. A legal or ethical question can arise near the Winter Solstice. Dedicate a candle ritual to peace and conflict resolution on the longest of nights.

Mercury favorably aspects Uranus January 1–4, promising breakthroughs in understanding. Technology, astrology and psychology figure into this progressive pattern. The remainder of January through early February is all about appreciating your heritage. The two most benefic planets, Venus and Jupiter, will join forces, brightening your sector of home, family and property then. Plan a house blessing at Imbolc, followed by a celebratory gathering.

On February 3 Venus joins Saturn and Pluto in your 5th house of love and pleasure. An attraction builds; romance is trending. A soul mate connection deepens near Valentine's Day. The last half of February through winter's end finds Mercury in opposition to your Sun. Others are anxious to share ideas. Listen carefully to gain valuable insights. Someone close by has old issues to resolve. The specifics are revealed after Mercury turns retrograde on March 5.

HEALTH
Uranus, ruler of your 6th house of health, begins a transit through Taurus this year. Innovative wellness programs and new medical research can intrigue you. The eclipse on July 27 accents health. Be aware of how your surroundings and associates affect your vitality near that time.

LOVE
Passionate, fiery Mars transits your love sector from the Vernal Equinox through May 15. An intimate relationship is quite consuming near May Eve. The eclipse on January 5 profoundly affects love connections and promises a significant turning point regarding tender sentiments.

SPIRITUALITY
Neptune is in the midst of a long transit through your 7th house of partnerships. This brings spiritual inspiration through associates. Accept invitations to visit a place of worship or spiritual circle. Encounters provide the catalyst for significant spiritual realizations. The defense rune *Eihwaz*, the Yew Tree, is linked to Virgo. It relates to interpreting blockages and delays as learning experiences, and generates perseverance and the ability to avert difficulties.

FINANCE
The Full Moon on March 31 falls in Libra, your 2nd house of finances. This finds you motivated to improve budgeting habits. July 10–September 8 brings a favorable Venus transit which first conjoins your Sun, then crosses into your money sector. Opportunities to add to earnings and shop for desired items come your way then.

LIBRA
September 23–October 23
Spring 2018–Spring 2019 for those
born under the sign of the Scales

A distinct charm and graciousness characterizes your interactions with others. Naturally genteel and hospitable, you strive to maintain harmony and goodwill in business and personal relationships alike. It can be difficult for you to make decisions because you so ardently desire to do right. Librans usually prefer companionship to a solitary lifestyle. You appreciate the fine arts, fashion, beauty and ornamentation of all kinds.

From the Vernal Equinox through All Fools Day, Venus, your ruler, opposes your Sun. Use humor and patience if encountering talented but volatile associates. During the first three weeks of April, Venus transits your 8th house. Messages from the afterlife bring peace and comfort. There are endings in progress; have faith that new beginnings are waiting in the wings. On May Eve plan a house blessing. Surprise those nearest and dearest with May baskets filled with candies and small tokens of love. Late May though mid-June finds a trio of transits in Gemini highlighting your 9th house. New studies and adventures will beckon. Different perspectives concerning your philosophical beliefs emerge. At the Summer Solstice a Venus transit in your 11th house heightens popularity. Both new and longtime friendships blossom during the longest and brightest summer days.

During the first three weeks of July the Sun transits your 10th house of career. This is competitive. Thoughts and conversations revolve around achieving greater success. A business trip, perhaps to attend a conference, can be rewarding. In early August, honor Lammas with an affirmation of gratitude for the blessings and abundance in your life. August 7–September 9 marks a bright and positive cycle. Venus transits Libra, bringing appreciation and rewards. Others are attracted by your allure and charm. By September 6 Saturn completes its retrograde in your home and family sector. Lingering concerns regarding housing and family dynamics will be examined by the Autumnal Equinox.

On September 23 the Sun joins Mercury in Libra. Your birthday accents travel and the exchange of information. Specific plans are finalized near the New Moon in Libra on October 8. Throughout October, Mars activates your 5th house. This favors creative projects and hobbies as well as sports and fitness programs. A loved one is adventurous and competitive. In the days just before Halloween, Venus conjoins Jupiter in Scorpio in your 2nd house. Explore antique or thrift shops to purchase vintage clothing. Assemble one-of-a-kind costumes for an autumn gala. Watch for unusual and collectible seasonal décor available for purchase as well. Photos or greeting cards from long ago surface to evoke happy memories. Smile as you place them on an ancestor altar. November 1–December 2 finds Venus revisiting Libra upon completing its retrograde cycle. This brings opportunities to do damage control regarding relationships or previously awkward social situations. It's an ideal time to change patterns and develop good habits. Accept and issue invitations. Social prospects are promising during November.

Early December finds Mars marching in conjunction with Neptune in your health sector. A dream or intuitive perception offers insights about wellness. A psychic bond with an animal companion strengthens during the weeks before the Winter Solstice. Mercury, Jupiter and the Sun will all highlight your 3rd house in mid-December. You'll feel restless and maybe even a bit bored. Travel during the winter holidays would present a novel change of pace. The first week of January finds you examining new options regarding living arrangements. A residential move is possible because the January 5 eclipse creates a stir in your 4th house. A mystery involving your heritage surfaces. From January 8 through Imbolc, Venus favorably aspects your Sun; good news arrives. Share anecdotes and jokes. Catch up on correspondence. Written affirmations and journaling help you implement worthwhile ideas. February begins with a Mars-Uranus pattern opposing your Sun. Others have expectations. Compromises are reached and tensions lessen after February 15. Transits in your 6th house help with getting organized and planning a healthy lifestyle during March.

HEALTH
The July 12 eclipse creates a stir in your 10th house of career and status and squares your Sun, which represents your vitality. This potent influence ripples throughout the rest of the year. It generates a need to maintain a wholesome, comfortable professional environment in order to maintain wellness.

LOVE
Mars, planet of passion and desire, ignites your love sector May 17–August 13 and again September 12–November 14. Admiration for a special someone grows and evolves. Share dreams and pursue projects together to deepen the bond. The eclipse on July 27 adds sparkle to your love life. Romance holds surprises during the late summer.

SPIRITUALITY
On August 11 and January 21 eclipses in your 11th house enhance the role organizations and friendships have in introducing new goals. This trend ushers in significant spiritual experiences linked to bettering the community as a whole. *Gebo*, the rune of partnership, is associated with Libra. Preserving personal freedom while balancing cooperation and maintaining equality is the spiritual influence it brings.

FINANCE
From the Vernal Equinox through November 7 lucky Jupiter blesses your 2nd house of earnings and cash flow. Cultivate promising financial opportunities then. The beneficial results will favorably affect your money matters for a long time to come. Retrograde Venus joins Jupiter in the financial sector during October. This also promises extra money, but do be careful not to overextend October 5–31.

SCORPIO
October 24 – November 21
Spring 2018 – Spring 2019 for those
born under the sign of the Scorpion

Outwardly rather reserved, the Scorpion is an enigma. Only occasionally is your inner maelstrom of emotional extremes, with strong opinions about everything and everyone, glimpsed by others. Mysteries are irresistible to you. You seek truth and probe beneath the surface to uncover raw facts. This includes exploring the eternal puzzles surrounding death, rebirth, reincarnation and the spirit world.

A touch of spring fever strikes at the Vernal Equinox. This malaise lingers through April while several transits affect your 6th house of health. Cleanse toxins from your body by drinking plenty of fresh water or juices and herbal teas to help boost your energy level. The Full Moon in Scorpio on April 29 conjoins Jupiter and has a refreshing effect. By May Eve you'll be attracted to study and travel. Try wildcrafting during May. Gather seasonal flowers and other plants as well as interesting stones as mementos of your adventures. Share a photo of your new treasures with like-minded friends. May 20 – June 12 finds Venus in Cancer, your sister water sign, brightening your 9th house. A program of study, perhaps involving a foreign language or philosophical topics, can pique your interest.

Shortly after the Summer Solstice Mars turns retrograde in your 4th house. This foreshadows some considerations regarding family life, property and residence. Examine past patterns regarding your domestic situation for deeper insight. The total lunar eclipse on July 27 brings the need to make some adjustments; a move could be planned. At Lammas focus on what must be blessed and released. Mercury and the Sun transit your sector of career and public life during August. Your thoughts turn toward new developments in your field. Colleagues offer inspiration. The New Moon on September 9 accents your 11th house. Dedication to improving the world around you, perhaps regarding ecology and animal welfare, brings personal satisfaction. The two benevolent planets, Venus and Jupiter, transit your sign from mid-September until Halloween. Focus on your personal appearance. New wardrobe items, hairstyles, etc. add to your charisma. An admirer draws near, and a favor is returned. During October music is a genuine source of solace and pleasure.

November 7 is a wonderful time to write a birthday wish list under the Scorpio New Moon. Set your intentions regarding the times to come. On November 15, Mars joins Neptune in your sector of love and pleasure. This sets the pace until January 1. Winter sports, creative Yuletide décor, planning social events and, of course, love connections can become very important near the Winter Solstice. This promises lifestyle improvements as well as the support and encouragement of others through early January. You'll make a favorable impression on the right people at holiday events. The eclipse on January 5 accents transportation needs. Make certain that vehicles are in good repair. Allow plenty of time if commuting to work. A coworker might be unable to complete a task in January. Your offer to help sparks a new friendship. The eclipse on January 21 accents some new career dynamics. Be receptive to growth and change. Adjustments could propel you into a different position. At Imbolc light a candle to bless your career concerns.

On February 10, Mercury joins Neptune in your 5th house, a favorable trend which lasts through winter's end. There is deeper communication with loved ones. An old flame might rekindle. This might involve shared dreams or other intuitive links. Imaginative ideas of genuine value develop. Make some notes about these to help you follow through in the future. After Mercury turns retrograde on March 5, inspirations can be easily forgotten. Winter's last days favor past life regression and meditation.

HEALTH
Volatile Mars rules your 6th house of health. Pace yourself when exercising. You might have a tendency to overdo it. The Mars retrograde June 26–August 27 is a time to focus on health goals. Take care of health needs January 1–February 13 when Mars makes a fated quincunx aspect to your Sun. Overall, Scorpios do tend to be long-lived survivors.

LOVE
Uranus will tickle the cusp of your 7th house before retrograding back into Aries May 15–November 5. Some surprises and excitement regarding intimate partnerships arise then. This time span foreshadows complex relationship situations which will change your love life over the next seven years. Venus will transit Scorpio promising happiness in love September 9–October 31 and again December 2–January 6.

SPIRITUALITY
On July 12 an eclipse affects your 9th house, the sector of higher thought and spiritual awakening. Spiritual experiences accelerate. New approaches to spirituality and encounters with new spiritual teachers can play a role in this. *Nauthiz,* the rune of constraint, relates to Scorpio. It stimulates spiritual growth through learning to handle limitations and challenges.

FINANCE
The year begins with benevolent Jupiter, ruler of your 2nd house of money, retrograde. Address old debts or other financial obligations. On July 11 Jupiter turns direct and then moves rapidly through Scorpio in conjunction with your Sun before beginning a year-long passage through your money sector on November 8. Congratulations. This is really favorable for finances. Opportunities arise this year which allow you to advance and more than meet your financial expectations and needs.

SAGITTARIUS
November 22–December 21
Spring 2018–Spring 2019 for those
born under the sign of the Archer

Energetic and enthusiastic, the Archer targets worthwhile goals and maintains a steady aim. Competitive situations and challenges bring out your brightest and best potentials. You are utterly sincere in expressing your thoughts and opinions. Unwittingly, you can bruise feelings of others though. Combine your intelligent chatter with a bit more tact. Then others will appreciate your cheerful companionship and ability to get things done.

Jupiter, your ruler, is retrograde as spring begins, making you uncharacteristically nostalgic and introspective. Reflect and remember while honoring the Vernal Equinox. The Full Moon on March 31 accents your 11th house, turning your attention to goals and networking. Mercury and the Sun join Uranus in your fellow fire sign of Aries during April. This is very social; a romantic involvement intensifies. A shared interest in a hobby, sport or creative project can lead to enjoyable times. Mid-May emphasizes health as transits affect your 6th house. Gather information about wellness and analyze options. Focus on diet and stress release. The Full Moon on May 29 in Sagittarius accents self awareness and reveals ways you can help yourself.

June 1–12 finds Mercury racing with the Sun in Gemini in an opposition aspect to you. Others voice ideas, and conversation is stimulating. As the Summer Solstice approaches, your sector of secrets and the afterlife is accented. Heed omens. Research of any kind is productive as June ends. The eclipse on July 12 focuses on your 8th house. Circumstances around inherited or invested money are in flux. Questions about insurance coverage or tax issues can be another consideration. Venus brightens your career sector from mid-July through August 5. Professional associates extend offers of friendship. A business conference or office party sets the scene for progress. At Lammas take time to savor the fruits of all you have accomplished. You'll feel adventurous and curious during mid to late August. Study programs are worthy of consideration as your 9th house is a focus. On August 28 ,Mars turns direct in your 2nd house of money where it will join Saturn. Financial realities are considered. Old financial obligations and choices affect your current situation from the end of August to mid-September. Be patient with budget constraints.

At the Autumnal Equinox, Mercury enters your 11th house where it remains until October 9. Friends present worthwhile ideas. You will be very interested in current events and inspired by new trends. The last part of October finds you cherishing privacy and secrets, as a stellium of transits burrows into your 12th house. Quiet acts of charity and time spent in contemplation can bring personal satisfaction. Answers come near Halloween when a longtime acquaintance appears and voices a new perspective concerning a situation from the past. In early November Jupiter begins a year-long passage through your 1st house. It's time to explore opportunities. Education and other types of self improvement captivate you as your birthday approaches. Home and family situations absorb your energy from November 16 through the end of December, while Mars transits your 4th house. Compromise helps; consult loved ones.

January accents cash flow and earning power. The eclipse on January 5 impacts your 2nd house. Focus on budgeting. Resist the temptation to take a financial risk or quit a job before another source of income is secured. January 8 through Imbolc finds Venus in Sagittarius. Love prevails. A variety of friends and enjoyable activities enrich your life. At Imbolc, brew a love potion and dedicate altar candles to igniting the heart's tender sentiments. On February 14, Mars enters your 6th house and remains through the winter season. Be patient with coworkers or employees. Mercury, the Sun and Neptune converge in your home and family sector during March. Relatives offer suggestions. Real estate or home improvements can be a hot topic. Try a house blessing or Feng Shui consultation soon after the New Moon on March 6.

HEALTH

Your 6th house of health is influenced by stubborn Taurus. Analyze how health habits, good or not, affect your well-being. On May 15, Uranus begins the first hint of a seven-year jaunt through Taurus. This shows that innovative technologies can bring worthy options regarding health care. This unusual transit provides opportunities to change your health and fitness regimes for the better.

LOVE

Your love sector is influenced by fiery Aries. A challenge and a bit of drama always adds color to romantic involvements. Passions can begin and end attachments quickly, especially if your freedom is at stake. The early spring, the week of the Full Moon on September 24, and early January through mid-February hold the promise of happiness in love.

SPIRITUALITY

The eclipses on August 11 and January 21 affect your 9th house of spiritual growth and the higher mind. Spiritual awakening is likely near those times. Your spirituality is evolving this year. *Kano* is your rune, a symbol which helps enhance spirituality. This is the thunderbolt of Thor or Jupiter, your ruler. It is an emblem of leadership and authority, giving the ability to take charge of situations and meet challenges.

FINANCE

Conservative Saturn, the ringed planet of parameters, edges slowly through your 2nd house of finances all year. Patience and attention to responsibilities bring rewards. This isn't the year to risk security. Instead embrace a solid work ethic. Carefully manage assets and seek bargains.

CAPRICORN
December 22 – January 19
Spring 2018 – Spring 2019 for those
born under the sign of the Goat

A calm, down-to-earth and deliberate quality characterizes Capricorns. Responsible, ambitious and well organized, you often have a flair for business. Conscientious, you win esteem and admiration for the way you keep things going while projecting faith and optimism. When work is done you often surprise others by displaying gourmet tastes and a subtle sense of humor.

As spring begins your focus is on completing projects. Energetic Mars joins serious Saturn in your sign until mid-May. Venus completes a transit in your 4th house of home and family March 20–31. Your residence can become a source of loving support and a haven. Late March–April 15 retrograde Mercury and the Sun bring visitors to your home. Look at repeating patterns and sift through memories to understand family dynamics. A positive Venus influence comes into play as May Eve approaches. The mood is relaxed, and there is time for love and leisure. The New Moon on May 15 favors vacation or party planning. Mercury's influence during the last half of May brings insight. Conversations with well informed associates provide a catalyst for expressing your own creative ideas.

During June transits in your 7th house of partnerships accent the accomplishments of one whom you're close to. Smile and bask in the glow of another's happiness and success. Dedicate the Summer Solstice to celebrating commitments and companionship. The Full Moon in your sign on June 28 illuminates choices regarding relationships. Mid-July through August 5 a Venus transit in Virgo, your 9th house, combines with favorable Uranus and Saturn transits. The languages and cultures of other lands, higher education and travel can all be a part of this. The August 11 eclipse activates your 8th house. The remainder of the month accents investigations, mysteries, the afterlife and managing assets.

On September 6, Saturn completes its retrograde, and Mars exits your 1st house a few days later. Nagging problems fade away; the outlook brightens. At the Autumnal Equinox there is news about your career. Business travel or a conference leads to an exceptional opportunity before the end of October. On October 23 the Sun joins Jupiter and Venus in your 11th house. The blessing of true friendship uplifts you during the rest of the month. Socialize and pursue wishes. Participation in charitable projects is satisfying at Halloween. During November, an opposition aspect between Venus in your 10th house and Uranus in your 4th house will find you juggling career demands with home and family life. There can be an unsettled quality. The secret to coping lies in time management and getting enough rest.

December begins with the Sun and Jupiter in your 12th house. Interpret dreams and jot down random thoughts. Intuitive flashes offer insights. The New Moon on December 7 clarifies the specifics. The Winter Solstice finds you seeking peace and privacy. Your birthday brings some intriguing comments and greetings. By January 1, Mars joins Uranus in your 4th house. A real estate transaction or household repair can be considered during the days ahead. Respect the opinions of family members. Someone is entering a new cycle and might want to break with the status quo at home. The eclipses on January 5 and 21 promise some fireworks during January. Your personal needs and financial planning can be keynotes. All that is certain is the need to change. Benevolent Venus enters Capricorn just after Imbolc to remain through February. Pressures ease and you'll find much to appreciate. A loved one reveals how much you are cherished. Go shopping for items you've longed for near the Full Moon on February 19.

During March some 3rd house transits, including Neptune, the Sun and Mercury, accent transportation and commuter travel. Purchasing a new vehicle can play a role in this. This trend also accents information exchange and imaginative ideas. As winter ends, listen. Others have important news to share.

HEALTH
Your 6th house of health is ruled by Mercury. Stay well informed about health factors in your environment. Discussions with a health care professional and friends or family can be helpful. The eclipse on January 5 in your sign accents your vitality. Study dietary measures or exercise programs to bolster wellness then.

LOVE
April and February are brightened by Venus transits which promote love. Uranus touches your love sector in May, bringing a hint of the lightning swift changes to come during the more distant future. The eclipse on July 12 falls in your 7th house of partnerships. This affects a partner's needs and choices regarding a close relationship. Flexibility on your part will nurture a bond.

SPIRITUALITY
Venus highlights your 9th house of spirituality during July. A loved one's faith can be a catalyst for spiritual awakening during the summer. Your rune is *Hagalaz*. Associated with winter storms, snow and hail, *Hagalaz* reveals how loss and disruption can lead to gain. Excessive focus on material security is restrictive. Balance it with spiritual values.

FINANCE
The July 27 eclipse in your 2nd house as well as the August 11 and January 21 eclipses in your 8th house augur changes in your source of income or financial strategy. The financial needs or income of a partner could impact your personal finances. Saturn, your ruler, is in your sign all year. This is a reminder about the work ethic. Keep patiently trying; rewards come in due time.

AQUARIUS
January 20–February 18
Spring 2018–Spring 2019 for those
born under the sign of the Water Bearer

A friendly dignity and enthusiasm for helping others characterizes Aquarius, sign of the humanitarian. Your curious nature inspires experimentation and inventiveness. You are an independent thinker, unconventional and always ready to challenge the status quo. Excessive displays of emotions and the expectations or demands of others can make you withdraw. You are a free spirit and prefer to keep your options open.

At the Vernal Equinox your ruler, Uranus, is joined by the Sun and Mercury in your 3rd house. The exchange of ideas and information and some short jaunts add variety to spring's early days. Prepare to juggle several projects simultaneously as April begins. Make time to entertain and beautify your residence when Venus brightens your home and family sector April 1–23. The Full Moon on April 29 finds you assuming new professional responsibilities. Emotions figure prominently in career aspirations. Dedicate May Eve rites to finding harmony through maintaining balance. Saturn and Pluto are both retrograde in your 12th house by early May, allowing you to put old regrets to rest. Forgiveness and forgetting offer the keys to serenity. It's time to create your own happiness. On May 16, Mars enters Aquarius where it remains for several months. A cycle of great accomplishment commences. Your motivation will carry you forward, as a highly competitive spirit prevails. June 1–11 a favorable Mercury influence aids in study, decision-making and productive travel. Your 5th house of love, leisure and creativity sets the pace until the Summer Solstice on June 21. This favors vacation plans and spending time with those whom you care for deeply.

July emphasizes fitness factors. Your 6th house of health sets the pace, with an eclipse on July 12 revealing the specifics. Mid-July finds animal companions uppermost in your heart and thoughts. An eclipse in Aquarius on July 27 brings elements of surprise. Adaptability will be helpful. At Lammas embrace your uniqueness. "There is but one of you in all of time" carry you forward into August. Retrograde Mercury in your 7th house of partnerships in August is ignited by the eclipse in Leo on August 11. Old patterns regarding relationships are in flux. Communicate and listen carefully.

September 1–10 several transits have you reflecting on your life's purpose. Take time to experience the healing, calming influences of nature. Earth elementals hover nearby. You can also sense the love and guidance of those who have passed into the spirit world. At the Autumn Equinox Mercury enters your 9th house, elevating your mental energy. Writing, study and philosophy are of interest. The New Moon on October 8 reveals the specifics. Travel is rewarding near Halloween too.

November 1–14 brings the last hurrah of a very long Mars transit in Aquarius. The momentum of your efforts propels you. Recent accomplishments involving career goals can set the pace for some time to come. During late November, retrograde Mercury joins Jupiter and the Sun in your 11th house. Longtime friendships are renewed. Participation in charitable and humanitarian endeavors brings satisfaction through the Winter Solstice. Late December finds Mars joining Neptune in your financial sector. Intuitive feelings or dreams revolve around security issues. Good or bad, all is not as it seems. Keep receipts, and monitor expense accounts.

January ushers in a restless mood. Your 3rd and 11th houses are highlighted. Concentration eludes you. You are mulling over goals and desires. On January 24, Mercury joins the Sun in your 1st house bringing understanding and clarity near your birthday. Include chanting, singing and storytelling in Imbolc rites. The New Moon on February 4 encourages expressing free will and independence. Mid-February turns your thoughts toward financial priorities; your 2nd house of cash flow and earnings is the focus. On March 1, Venus enters Aquarius where it attracts happiness and fulfillment through the rest of the winter.

HEALTH
Exercise is very helpful in maintaining wellness while Mars transits your birth sign May 16–August 12 and again September 11–November 14. The July 12 eclipse in your health sector accents new dietary and health care options. Monitor changes in your health over the summer. Consider having a general checkup.

LOVE
Loyalties and commitments are in flux this year. Two eclipses, on July 27 and January 21, shake up your 7th house of relationships. Expect changes and growth regarding intimate partnerships. Venus comes to the rescue, beaming with favorable influences April 24–May 18 and again as winter ends.

SPIRITUALITY
Your 9th house of spirituality is ruled by sociable Libra. Friendships with like-minded companions uplift you spiritually. The Full Moon on March 31 ushers in a time of spiritual awakening. The rune *Laguz*, which means "fluidity and water," is your spiritual symbol. Flowing with circumstances that feel comfortable and heeding intuition are its message. *Laguz* has a cleansing influence, culminating in an alchemical transformation and happy endings.

FINANCE
Uranus hovers on the cusp of practical, security-oriented Taurus from mid-May through early November. This foreshadows changing financial situations, especially regarding family needs and real estate issues. Events then hint at the overall direction of finances during the next seven years. Be alert to opportunities for professional expansion leading to more financial acumen while Jupiter influences your 10th house of career March 21–November 7.

PISCES
February 19–March 20
Spring 2018–Spring 2019 for those
born under the sign of the Fish

Impressionable, generous, trusting and sensitive, you reflect the emotional nuances in your environment. Elude negative people and places in order to quell turmoil by association. Your dreams are vivid and meaningful. Interpreting them brings guidance from the higher consciousness. Your optimism and ability to create a calming influence give you great healing and problem-solving capabilities.

At the Vernal Equinox the Sun enters your 2nd house of finances and aspects Mars in your sector of wishes and friendships. Early spring finds a friend offering business advice or perhaps seeking a loan. Listen and reflect, but don't be overly generous. Share only what you can afford to risk. April 1–23 Venus favorably highlights your 3rd house. Creative ideas and pleasant conversation enable you to charm others. A neighborhood gathering strengthens valuable relationships. Late April through May 12, Mercury joins Uranus in your financial sector. Original ideas involve ways to generate extra income. You'll value money for the freedom it can bring.

From late May through mid-June, Venus trines your Sun, supporting creative and artistic ventures while fostering enjoyment of hobbies. June 13–28 brings a favorable Mercury aspect into play. Pursue travel opportunities; accept invitations. Greeting cards and notes speak volumes. Be a good listener. Write affirmations at the Summer Solstice. At the end of June, Mars turns retrograde in your 12th house. An introspective mood prevails during the long, warm summer days. Cherish quiet reverie. By Lammas your health sector is active. Try a foot massage or breathing exercises to enhance vitality. Late August through the first week of September several powerful transits, including Mars, occur in your 11th house. Assertive friends mean well but can be insistent in having you participate in social activities, perhaps involving an organization. Cooperate if this is enjoyable, but back off if you start to feel overwhelmed. September 10–Halloween, Venus is in your sector of philosophy and higher learning. Creative ideas, perhaps involving a writing project, occupy your thoughts. Spiritual art, poetry and music compliment Halloween celebrations.

Mercury hovers in your 10th house of career throughout November. There may be some rumors afoot. Check sources for validity amid startling news. A chance to travel through your work is likely. Mars enters Pisces by November 16 where it ushers in a dynamic cycle which remains in force through December. Neptune, your ruler, turns direct on November 24. Your energy level is high and much can be accomplished. Take the lead; others respond to your influence. The New Moon on December 7 conjoins Jupiter in your 10th house. This is favorable, attracting recognition and opportunities for career growth. Be optimistic and look at the broader picture. At the Winter Solstice, Venus is favorably aspected in your 9th house. Seasonal art, music and literature forge a connection with the spiritual tone of the season. Plan a holiday gathering and set the mood by simmering a stove-top incense including pine and cinnamon.

January accents your 11th house. Friends include you in plans. Expect a request for assistance. A community project or political agenda might play a role. The eclipse on January 5 reveals the specifics. Previous plans are revamped by the end of the month. As Imbolc nears, your 12th house sets the pace. Trust your instincts. Dreams and hunches bring subconscious longings and intuitive messages to the surface. On February 10, Mercury enters Pisces where it remains through winter's end. You'll feel a vague restlessness and would enjoy a change of pace. Participate in studies, discussion groups and travel. Near your birthday Uranus joins Mars in your 3rd house. Neighborhood improvements and relationships with siblings impact your outlook. Be optimistic concerning changes and new ideas which are presented. The week of the New Moon on March 6 highlights the specifics.

HEALTH
Temperature extremes affect your health, which is ruled by Leo and the Sun. Wear sunglasses, hats and lotions to protect your skin from the wind and glare. Warm socks and sweaters are winter essentials. Two eclipses, one on August 11 and the other on January 21, impact your health sector. Consider cardiovascular exercise and take note of changes in your health this year. New health care professionals offer perspectives.

LOVE
Your 5th house of romance is accented by a promising Venus transit May 19–June 13. Loved ones express caring admiration then. Enhance a cherished relationship with a walk by the sea or a romantic, home-cooked dinner. Include spring flowers and a bottle of nice champagne. The eclipse on July 12 is revealing and profoundly affects the direction of an intimate relationship.

SPIRITUALITY
Perth, the rune of initiation and secrets, has a special spiritual significance for you. It has a transformative, phoenix-like energy. Unexpected, powerful forces of change leading to a new dawn rising from the ashes of a dark night of the soul is the message. Step outside the confines of the ordinary to cultivate new opportunities. Planetary transits from Halloween through early January activate your sector of spirituality. Meditate during the dark and quiet evening hours then for spiritual guidance.

FINANCE
Erratic and impatient Uranus is now exiting your financial sector, where it has hovered for several years. Finances gradually become more stable between May and November and again from March 7 onward. Bless a prosperity talisman on your May Eve altar. Monitor how partnerships affect your security during the late summer and autumn months.

Sites of Awe

Safed, Israel

AFTER SOME TIME—I have always wanted to visit Israel's sacred sites—I came across the opportunity to travel with a group of friends and family to northern Israel, to the sacred city of Safed (sometimes called Safet). As our tour bus takes us up and down the hills, I recall the guide book describing this rather small town, located in the farthest northern part of Israel as being almost 3000 feet above sea level, having views of mountainous regions and of the Sea of Galilee.

The tour guide continued to explain that Safed became a spiritual center in the 16th century, when many Jewish mystics and scholars settled here, bringing with them Jewish mysticism known as Kabbalah (or Cabala) which was once a well-kept secret, even to most Israelis.

As our bus driver begins to slow down, he comes to a fork in the narrow road, turning into a parking lot—a dry, dirt space with very little room for our large tour bus. Our guide has just explained that we have two hours to explore. Hum. I don't think this is enough time for someone with my interest in Kabbalah, but I will give it my best. Safed is one of the four holy cities in Israel and I want to explore this center street to its fullest. I guess I will be doing an abridged version of what I really want to do.

Here in the old part of town, the streets are narrow and paved with cobblestones. I think it would be best to jog down this street and look both ways to get a broad view of what there is to see. Once I get to the end of this central street, I will make my way back. This will make it easier

to reach the bus on time. I almost missed the bus at Masada!

My goal is to find a nice Tree of Life charm or necklace. I prefer sterling silver, but will take whatever I can get since the stingy tour guide only gave me 2 hours to cover this magnificent street, lined with ancient synagogues, restaurants, private homes on several levels, gift shops, art galleries and cafes.

As I quickly make my way down the street, I see some wonderful gift shops—some with jewelry in the window. I will be sure to find what I am looking for. A little out of breath, very warm and extremely anxious, I have reached the end of this ancient and very beautiful street lined in various forms of art. And this is not even the artist quarter of the city, just one street in the Old City area of Safed.

Time to turn back and investigate!
There is a sign for Torah study in a shop window. I can only imagine how much easier it would be to study here in this mountainous region—the air is clean and the environment is so very serene. And there is a building with another Torah sign in the window. It looks a little like a religious building and a little like a library as well. I'm going to step in to see what it is. It is a little dark in here and the smell of incense is heavy. The feeling is amazing and difficult to describe. Old, yes, very old, but continuous. Ongoing and persevering energy that changes very little through the ages—timeless. There is a rabbi lecturing and about 25 people sitting on the floor around him. Most are just listening, but a couple of them are taking notes as he speaks. I'll stand here in the back of the room with my back to the stone wall. The wall is cool, and I briefly wonder how many other people have stood here over the centuries listening to the most religious and mystical of teachers in Israel. Oops, in my daydreaming I did not notice the rabbi is looking rather annoyed at me . . . time to leave. I slip along the back

wall and try to leave without making a sound—nope, the door is very creaky. Now most of the students turn their heads in my direction. I smile, nod and extend my apologies as I exit as quickly as possible. It is funny that when you are enamored by the magic of mysticism and ancient knowledge, you pay very little attention to the needs of man.

After going through several jewelry stores, I have not been able to find a Tree of Life pendant. Everyone keeps showing me small images of trees with branches and leaves. The Tree of Life, at least for the tourists, seems to have evolved into just images of trees. I'm not happy about this, so I will keep looking. Even the gift shops are selling window seals of trees, lamps in the shape of trees and other gifts with tree-images on them.

Well, this place looks hopeful. It seems a little more old-fashioned than the other shops. Asking yet another clerk about a tree of life pendant, she shows me even more images of botanical trees. I shrug my shoulders and say "Thank you, anyway."

The pleasant woman behind the counter asks, "Are you looking for something else?" After explaining that I wanted the Tree of Life as a symbol of Kabbalistic study, she held her index finger up and smiled. Reaching down under the counter, she takes out a small tray that has a selection of pendants—most of them the Tree of Life—some with colored stones marking the Sephiroth, some more simple. "I'll take this one," pointing to a plain sterling piece.

I'm very happy with my purchase, now to run and catch the bus!

Safed is a charming, serene and beautiful city filled with wonder. All around you can feel a connection with mysticism and sacred lore. But, visitors are challenged by the façade of post cards, gifts and souvenirs. Should you be lucky enough to visit this holy city, be sure to spend time to feel its essence, and pray that the city opens the doors to the hidden secrets that lace its magnificent history.

—ARMAND TABER

The Balsam Fir
A Useful Spiritual Gift from the Forest

AMONG THE ICONIC SYMBOLS of Yuletide, the balsam fir is especially treasured as a traditional generator of good cheer and holiday spirit. This lovely species of coniferous fir is plentiful around the Great Lakes region of the United States. Balsam flourishes among the thick lowland forests, bogs and wetlands of Wisconsin and Upper Michigan, sharing the moist soil and humidity with tamarack and spruce. It is said among the Native Americans that the boughs of the balsam fir, called Nimisse, will sacrifice their wonderful fragrance as an offering to The Great Spirit to bless those who can't pray for themselves. This suggests balsam is a forerunner of the aromatherapy treatments so popular today among those who prefer alternative health care.

A traditional legend about the balsam involves a father with several small children. One long and cold winter the family was very hungry, even close to starvation. The father went out ice fishing, desperate to bring home something to eat. He eventually caught the biggest fish he had ever seen. The deeply spiritual and grateful man wanted to stop to thank The Great Spirit, but he feared the big fish would be lost. As he struggled to hold on and bring it in, he called out to Nimisse. The balsam fir heard his pleas and used its fragrance to make an offering of thanksgiving on his behalf.

In addition to wreaths, the ubiquitous Yuletide symbol of the unbroken circle honoring the cycle of the seasons, the balsam boughs are also crafted into crosses. Their fragrance is thought to smooth the path to the afterlife. In the North these balsam crosses are placed

along roadways. It is said they bring comfort to the souls of those who have perished in auto accidents, often related to drunk driving.

Recently a CD-Rom titled "Onjiakiing" was recorded by The Great Lakes Indian Fish and Wildlife Commission (GLIFWC) for the purpose of documenting traditional knowledge and preserving it for future generations. The CD mentions a number of practical and spiritual applications for indigenous plants, including healing. An elder from Michigan known among the Native Americans as Keewaydinoquay speaks fondly of the balsam in the Ojibwa language. Keewaydinoquay tells of her childhood and says the name Nimisse means "elder sister." She reveals how balsam was highly respected for the prayerful fragrance it gives up on behalf of all. Additionally the pitch from the balsam tree is good to treat burns, to use as a chewing gum and a sealant. The balsam saplings can be fashioned into particularly good fence posts and lodge supports. When maple sugar season comes, a branch of balsam placed in the boiling sap cuts down on the foam and helps to create a superior syrup.

— MARINA BRYONY

Reviews

The Witching Herbs: 13 Essential Plants and Herbs for Your Magical Garden
Harold Roth
ISBN-13: 978-1578635993
Weiser Books
$18.95

HAROLD ROTH'S FIRST foray into the world of printed publishing has generated quite a bit of hubbub among mystical communities, particularly those which focus on Traditional Craft, Verdant Gnosis and the Poison Path. Granted, anyone familiar with his wildly popular alchemy-works.com website is generally nonplussed by this, due to a solid reputation of being one of the most reliable mail-order herb, oil, incense and seed websites for the past 17 years.

It is due to the above that this volume has been endorsed quite a bit this past year in the world of Witchcraft and its related disciplines, with blogs and social media sites abound singing Roth's praises and taking pictures of the book's gracefully-illustrated mandrake cover. All the hype is well-deserved.

This is not due to any radical new theories concerning the herbal path, nor from any bizarre, never-before-seen ritual uses of the thirteen plants discussed, but instead the glowing accolades come from finding a well-researched, engaging, easily digestible and no-nonsense liber of herbal lore and practice. From witchy staples like Mugwort and Wormwood, to more dangerous denizens like Henbane and Belladonna, one would be hard-pressed to find a more affable and inviting guide to the Greenwood path.

Though each chapter dedicates a considerable amount of space to the legends and folklore associated with the plants in question, *The Witching Herbs* is still very much a "doers" manual, with practical advice, recipes and tricks of the trade garnered from years of trial, error and reward. Roth's writing style is conversational, yet chock full of important tips and details many similar books might skip over if not downright ignore. If pitfalls exist, he will not hesitate to warn the reader and steer them clear of imminent danger and frustration — especially important since most of the herbs covered are toxic and/or downright deadly if misused — while leading them toward fulfilling herbal experiences without the fear of a surprise hospital visit.

Keys to Perception: A Practical Guide to Psychic Development
Ivo Dominguez, Jr.
ISBN-13: 978-1578636204
Weiser Books
$18.95

IT'S ALWAYS a pleasant surprise when an understated title unfolds into a powerful and intelligible reading experience.

Dozens of books claiming to be like this one come out every year, but usually devolve into the flimsy essays of armchair theoreticians.

In contrast, each chapter of *Keys to Perception* is positively brimming with practical exercises of memory work, pathworking and active visualization. Each activity is interwoven with its philosophical basis, from basic elemental energies and shielding to more complicated psychic structures.

Of particular note is Dominguez' clever variation of the classic Middle Pillar ritual, utilizing Qabalistic concepts to expand the rite into both a circle casting as well as a means of awakening the chakras. Also included is one of the most grounded primers on the use of crystals and stones one may be able to find. Ultimately, experience and the wisdom gained from it shines through every page of this graceful little codex. Definitely recommended.

Santa Muerte: The History, Rituals, and Magic of Our Lady of the Holy Death
Tracey Rollin
ISBN-13: 978-1578636211
Weiser Books
$16.95

THE MYSTERIOUS FOLK Saint, Santa Muerte, has been growing in popularity over recent decades, with an incredibly varied host of devotees. Catholics, Pagans, Satanists, Hermeticists and many more mystics in-between have been creating shrines in her honor. Though much about her is shrouded in mystery, much of her radiant glory is revealed through this inciteful number.

Witch and Chaos Magician Tracey Rollin's newest effort is as much a grimoire as it is a philosophical treatise on the worship of this much-misunderstood matron. The first four chapters give a fascinating glimpse into the history and folklore associated with the beloved saint, from her Aztec roots to her reverence and worship in Mexico, South America and beyond. By Chapter Five: "The Seven Colors of Santa Muerte," the text transforms into a straight-up book of magic, with spells, rites, chants, prayers and offerings galore. Like a true Chaote, Rollin leaves a fair amount of wiggle room for each individual practitioner to tailor their rites as they see fit, while simultaneously getting down to the nitty-gritty of spellwork with clarity and ease.

Odin: Ecstasy, Runes, & Norse Magic
Diana L. Paxson
ISBN-13: 978-1578636105
Weiser Books
$22.95

THE MYSTERIES OF Old One-Eye are vast and ancient. Though the All-father of the Norse people was generally viewed as a Lord of wisdom and magic, much more has been connected to his rites and name-sake over the centuries. Diana Paxson takes the reader on a very personal journey of Odin's evolution throughout the ages, from the shamanic trances of his priests and his presence in the Eddas and the Havamal, all the way through to his influence upon the writings of Tolkien, Gaiman and Marvel Comics.

With constant references to the various Scandinavian legends and folktales, Paxson helps to reveal the considerable depth to this many-faced deity, weaving rune spells and poetic rites drawn from or inspired by Odin's character within. Whether studying the Desired One, the Rider of the Tree, or the God of Death, the reader is treated to beautiful rituals and rich stories of Northern magic.

The Magical Art of Crafting Charm Bags: 100 Mystical Formulas for Success, Love, Wealth and Wellbeing
Elohim Leafar
ISBN-13: 978-1578636198
Weiser Books
$16.95

PRECISELY WHAT IT claims to be and then some. Leafar has created one of the handiest little manuals of charm-bag creation one will hope to open. No frills or filler, but lots of wonderful recipes and combinations. For those new to herb and root work, this book acts as an ideal primer, and for those with far more experience beneath their proverbial belts, this book will be a breath of inspiration if one is having trouble deciding the perfect spell component or incense ingredient.

The first section of the book dedicates itself to some general preliminaries concerning circles, altars and incenses, but then it's off to the races (or craft table). In truth, *The Magical Art of Crafting Charm Bags* feels less like a grimoire and far more like magical cookbook without the actual cooking (except maybe in a few select cases). Leafar marches out recipe after recipe, combination after combination, all while engagingly explaining the folklore associated with each ingredient. Stones, bones, oils and herbs reveal themselves to be far less intimidating than they may have original appeared.

A solid addition to the occult library no matter what path one might be following.

Esoteric Empathy: A Magickal & Metaphysical Guide to Emotional Sensitivity
Raven Digitalis
ISBN-13: 978-0738749174
Llewellyn Publications
$19.99

SOME OF US HAVE been in the occult game for a long time, and have heard the word "empathy" so often it makes us twitch, especially when uttered by a nearby youngling who seems to be preening more than practicing, so to speak. However, if said youngling is referring to this book, rest at ease. And be jealous.

Esoteric Empathy will leave many of us who began our occult training decades ago, to wish a book like this had come out "back in the day." Not only does it go over the simplest (but of course, most crucial) basics of dealing with esoteric and emotional sensitivity (as well as their darker manifestations such as addiction and dependency) but it is chock-bloody-full of exercises, meditations, spells and chants from various disciplines, each designed to hone and train the will and sensitivity of the practitioner.

Scientific empathy studies and mass-media concerns are folded and wedded with Buddhist and Hindu mantras, hand mudras, Qabalistic pathworkings, energetic shielding practices, sigils and correspondences a-plenty. It is kind without coddling and informs without judgement or dragging out a point. *Esoteric Empathy* is simply a psychic self-defense handbook par excellence. Recommended for preening younglings, twitching elders and all practitioners in between.

The Carmichael Watson Project
http://www.carmichaelwatson.lib.ed.ac.uk/cwatson/

THE HIGHLANDS of Scotland are world-renowned for their breathtaking vistas and jagged, windy coasts. To Witches, historians, anthropologists and occultists they have also been treasure-troves of legends, folklore, eldritch ruins, Neolithic stone circles and ancient tumuli. Its residents have been spinning tales of banshees, selkies, brownies and other denizens of the Fey realms for centuries. The Gaelic language—still studied and spoken there—is rich with poetry and magic. It is said one could study the Highlands for a lifetime and still find new tales and ancient sites yet to be discovered.

Conveniently, there was a person who indeed spent their lifetime studying the rich heritage of northern Scotland and the Hebrides, who learned various dialects and collected volumes of Gaelic custom and lore. His name was Alexander Carmichael (1832–1912), and his anthology of Hebridean ballads, charms and chants, *Carmina Gadelica*, is still deemed one of the most important collections of Celtic folklore today.

The University of Edinburgh has recently created a user-friendly website of Carmichael's extensive library, notes and manuscripts, opening his life's work to students of all disciplines interested in the legends and mysteries of northern and western Scotland. Deemed the "foremost collection of its kind in the country," the dauntingly large database includes indexes, handwriting manuals and geographic guides to make one's browsing advance more smoothly. Hours of easily-searchable wisdom await.

Balkan Traditional Witchcraft
Radomir Ristic (translated by Michael C. Carter, Jr.)
ISBN-13: 978-0979616853
Pendraig Publishing
$19.95

THE ENGLISH-READING world has been given a great treasure in this translation of Radomir Ristic's seminal work on Witchcraft in the Balkan Territories. This astute and cogent book feels like the grimoire an anthropologist wrote, teaching the reader the philosophies behind the many folk magic traditions of Croatia, Bosnia, Serbia, Slovenia and even parts of Russia (to a lesser extent), while revealing field notes and old stories connected to each practice or magical tool. Fascinating fables and spells of the 'Dragon Men,' cunning folk and Vlach Witches are coupled with practical protection spells, love charms, herbal advice and divinations.

Though much will be new to readers of the mystical arts, much will feel very familiar, as the traditions of the Balkans resonate easily with the magical work of other nations and landscapes. The sanctity of rivers and streams, the use of brooms, cauldrons and black-handled knives, group folk-dances for fertility and bounty, the reverence toward ancestors and spirits of the land. All these reveal the timelessness and pervasiveness of the 'Old Ways' as a whole, while simultaneously revealing the unique flourishes and perspectives our Eastern European friends bring toward the practice of natural magic.

Peace of mind

What is the best way to prepare for a ritual?—Submitted by Madeline Bartell

There are probably as many ways to prepare for ritual as there are moments in a day. The common denominator in all is there must be time in which to bring your body and mind into a clean and calm state. Most will begin their process a few hours before the actual ritual. Limiting the amount and type of food you eat is a good start. Heavy meals can create a tired mind and ground your energy. Closer to the ritual, taking a shower and ritual bath will help to clear both physical and psychic dirt. You can add herbs (such as hyssop) and oils (vervain is lovely) to the bath to settle the psyche. Lastly, you should take a bit of time to ground and center before beginning. Rhythmic breathing will do much to affect the shift that you may need.

What's in a name

What is the best way to choose a magical name and when should I choose one?—Submitted by Tom Gallo

Choosing a magical name or a magical motto is a common practice among Pagans, Witches and Magicians. At birth we are given a name by our parents. We choose a name in the magical community to more accurately reflect our demeanor and our aspirations. It is because of these implications that a name should be chosen with care. There isn't really a rule as to when you should assume a name. To choose a name, you will want to do a bit of research and think hard. We recommend that it not be a name that is "too big," as you will grow into the name over time. For example, you might not want to use a name such as Thánatos, the God who brought on death indiscriminately. If shepherding folks through the process of death, perhaps a psychopomp such as Hermes or Chairon might be a better choice. Choosing a motto might be an easier choice since this is indicative of where you want to go or aspire to.

The naked truth

Do I have to take my clothes off to be effective in my rituals?—Submitted by Janet Anderson

There are a few traditions in Witchcraft that practice nudity, usually known as "skyclad." There are many genuine reasons why a group might require ritual nudity. Key amongst the reasons is that nudity is a natural state of being. We come into the world bearing our bum for all to see. Also, many believe that nudity creates a sense of freedom and equanimity. It is difficult to hide behind the artifice of social station when you don't have the trappings the indicate status. There are many groups that do not require nudity, rather they require that you have a robe of a specific color. Our best advice is go with your gut. If you are practicing solitary, do what is comfortable and natural for you. If you intend on joining a group, this might be a question that you should ask in the interview.

Are you equipped?

Should I make my own ritual equipment or is store bought OK?—Submitted by Toni Acevedo

Making your own tools can be both gratifying and frustrating. The act of fabrication will invariably imbue the object with your own sentiment and power. Some of the tools that you use during a ritual are easy to make and others require a great amount of skill. A ritual dagger requires that you have an ability to access and use a forge. Making a bowl to hold water and other elements will of course take less effort. If your intent is to make your tools, do a good amount of research and have patience.

For those who are not inclined to make their own tools, don't despair. Buying ritual equipment is common and can be equally fun. While you can buy great "witchy looking" things, you can also look for equipment in your local antique and second hand shops. One bit of advice, if you do buy it make sure that you put it through a ritual cleansing. You don't want to drag along unnecessary psychic ick into your well-cleansed circle.

All those in favor...

Should I divine before every bit of magic that I do?—Submitted by Gale Moch

The short answer is no. If you are unsure of whether you should do a given working, you should definitely do some sort of divination to suggest yay or nay.

Let us hear from you, too

We love to hear from our readers. Letters should be sent with the writer's name (or just first name or initials), address, daytime phone number and e-mail address, if available. Published material may be edited for clarity or length. All letters and e-mails will become the property of The Witches' Almanac Ltd. *and will not be returned. We regret that due to the volume of correspondence we cannot reply to all communications.*

The Witches' Almanac, Ltd.
P.O. Box 1292
Newport, RI 02840-9998
info@TheWitchesAlmanac.com
www.TheWitchesAlmanac.com

194

DAME FORTUNE'S WHEEL TAROT
A PICTORIAL KEY
PAUL HUSON

The Witches' Almanac presents:

- *Illustrates for the first time, traditional Tarot card interpretations unadorned by the occult speculations of Mathers, Waite or Crowley.*

- *Expounds on the meanings collected by Jean-Baptiste Alliette, a Parisian fortune-teller otherwise known as Etteilla*

Based upon Paul Huson's research in Mystical Origins of the Tarot, Dame Fortune's Wheel Tarot illustrates for the first time the earliest, traditional Tarot card interpretations as collected in the 1700s by Jean-Baptiste Alliette In addition to detailed descriptions full color reproductions of Huson's original designs for all 79 cards are provided, including an extra Significator card as specified by Etteilla that may be used optionally. 200 pages $19.95

For information visit TheWitchesAlmanac.com/dame-fortunes-wheel-tarot-a-pictorial-key/

MAGIC

An Occult Primer

David Conway

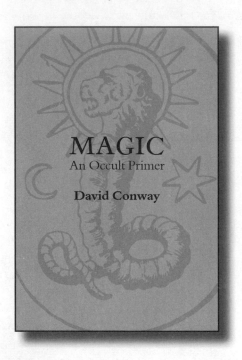

The Witches' Almanac Coloring Book

Gwion Vran and
Ydal Nevrom

The Witches' Almanac presents:

• *96 Black and white images for coloring.*

• *A brief introduction to the contents of each section.*

• *Historic woodcuts and 22 Major Arcana and the four Aces of the Tarot.*

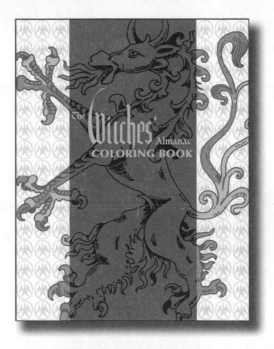

The Witches' Almanac has long featured black and white images of beautiful woodcuts, fantastical creatures, tarot cards, astrological features and constellations, as well as line drawing selected from the folklore of our global community. The Witches' Almanac Coloring Book brings together a lager format of these images presented in past Almanacs (in addition to images that have not been presented) allowing the inner artist to emerge in a mediation of color.

112 pages — $12.00

For further information visit http://TheWitchesAlmanac.com/

Aradia
Gospel of the Witches
Charles Godfrey Leland

ARADIA IS THE FIRST work in English in which witchcraft is portrayed as an underground old religion, surviving in secret from ancient pagan times.

• Used as a core text by many modern neo-pagans.

• Foundation material containing traditional witchcraft practices

• This special edition features appreciations by such authors and luminaries as Paul Huson, Raven Grimassi, Judika Illes, Michael Howard, Christopher Penczak, Myth Woodling, Christina Oakley Harrington, Patricia Della-Piana, Jimahl di Fiosa and Donald Weiser. A beautiful and compelling work, this edition has brought the format up to date, while keeping the text unchanged. 172 pages $16.95

⋙ Expanded classics! ⋘
The ABC of Magic Charms
Elizabeth Pepper

SINCE THE DAWN of mankind, an obscure instinct in the human spirit has sought protection from mysterious forces beyond mortal control. Human beings sought benefaction in the three realms that share Earth with us — animal, mineral, vegetable. All three, humanity discovered, contain mysterious properties discovered over millennia through occult divination. An enlarged edition of *Magic Charms from A to Z*, compiled by the staff of *The Witches' Almanac.* $12.95

The Little Book of Magical Creatures
Elizabeth Pepper and Barbara Stacy
A loving tribute to the animal kingdom

AN UPDATE of the classic *Magical Creatures*, featuring Animals Tame, Animals Wild, Animals Fabulous – plus an added section of enchanting animal myths from other times, other places. *A must for all animal lovers.* $12.95

✤ a lady shape-shifts into a white doe ✤ two bears soar skyward
✤ Brian Boru rides a wild horse ✤ a wolf growls dire prophecy

The Witchcraft of Dame Darrel of York

Charles Godfrey Leland

Introduction by Robert Mathiesen

The Witches' Almanac presents:

- *A previously unpublished work by folklorist Charles Godfrey Leland.*
- *Published in full color facsimile with a text transcript.*
- *Forward by Prof. Robert Mathiesen.*

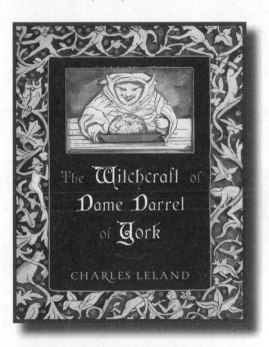

This beautifully reproduced facsimile of the illuminated manuscript will shed light on an ancient tradition as well as provide the basis for a modern practice. It will be treasured by those practicing Pagans, scholars and all those fascinated by the legend and lore of England.

Standard hardcover edition ($65.00).
Deluxe numbered edition with slipcase ($85.00).
Exclusive full leather bound, numbered and slip cased edition ($145.00).

For information visit TheWitchesAlmanac.com/the-witchcraft-of-dame-darrel-of-york/

The products and services offered above are paid advertisements.

❧ MARKETPLACE ❧

TO: The Witches' Almanac
P.O. Box 1292, Newport, RI 02840-9998
www.TheWitchesAlmanac.com

Name_____

Address_____

City_____ State_____ Zip_____

E-mail_____

WITCHCRAFT being by nature one of the secretive arts, it may not be as easy to find us next year. If you'd like to make sure we know where you are, why don't you send us your name and address? You will certainly hear from us.

ANCIENT ROMAN HOLIDAYS

The glory that was Rome awaits you in Barbara Stacy's classic presentation of a festive year in pagan times. Here are the gods and goddesses as the Romans conceived them, accompanied by the annual rites performed in their worship. Scholarly, light-hearted – a rare combination.

CELTIC TREE MAGIC

Robert Graves in *The White Goddess* writes of the significance of trees in the old Celtic lore. *Celtic Tree Magic* is an investigation of the sacred trees in the remarkable Beth-Luis-Nion alphabet; their role in folklore, poetry and mysticism.

MOON LORE

As both the largest and the brightest object in the night sky, and the only one to appear in phases, the Moon has been a rich source of myth for as long as there have been mythmakers.

MAGIC SPELLS AND INCANTATIONS

Words have magic power. Their sound, spoken or sung, has ever been a part of mystic ritual. From ancient Egypt to the present, those who practice the art of enchantment have drawn inspiration from a treasury of thoughts and themes passed down through the ages.

LOVE FEASTS

Creating meals to share with the one you love can be a sacred ceremony in itself. With the witch in mind, culinary adept Christine Fox offers magical menus and recipes for every month in the year.

RANDOM RECOLLECTIONS
II, III, IV

Pages culled from the original (no longer available) issues of *The Witches' Almanac*, published annually throughout the 1970's, are now available in a series of tasteful booklets. A treasure for those who missed us the first time around; keepsakes for those who remember.

A Treasury from past editions...

Perfect for study or casual reading, Witches All *is a collection from* The Witches' Almanac *publications of the past. Arranged by topics, the book, like the popular almanacs, is thought provoking and often spurs me on to a tangent leading to even greater discovery. The information and art in the book – astrological attributes, spells, recipes, history, facts & figures is a great reminder of the history of the Craft, not just in recent years, but in the early days of the Witchcraft Revival in this century: the witch in an historical and cultural perspective.*   Ty Bevington, Circle of the Wicker Man, Columbus, Ohio

Absolutely beautiful! I recently ordered Witches All *and I have to say I wasn't disappointed. The artwork and articles are first rate and for a longtime* Witches' Almanac *fan, it is a wonderful addition to my collection.* Witches' Almanac *devotees and newbies alike will love this latest effort. Very worth getting.*
                                                            Tarot3, Willits, California

GREEK GODS IN LOVE

Barbara Stacy casts a marvelously original eye on the beloved stories of Greek deities, replete with amorous oddities and escapades. We relish these tales in all their splendor and antic humor, and offer an inspired storyteller's fresh version of the old, old mythical magic.

MAGIC CHARMS FROM A TO Z

A treasury of amulets, talismans, fetishes and other lucky objects compiled by the staff of *The Witches' Almanac.* An invaluable guide for all who respond to the call of mystery and enchantment.

LOVE CHARMS

Love has many forms, many aspects. Ceremonies performed in witchcraft celebrate the joy and the blessings of love. Here is a collection of love charms to use now and ever after.

MAGICAL CREATURES

Mystic tradition grants pride of place to many members of the animal kingdom. Some share our life. Others live wild and free. Still others never lived at all, springing instead from the remarkable power of human imagination.

BRACELETS			
Item	Price	Qty.	Total
Agate, Green	$5.95		
Agate, Moss	$5.95		
Agate, Natural	$5.95		
Agate, Red	$5.95		
Aventurine	$5.95		
Fluorite	$5.95		
Jade, African	$5.95		
Jade, White	$5.95		
Jasper, Picture	$5.95		
Jasper, Red	$5.95		
Malachite	$5.95		
Onyx, Black	$5.95		
Quartz Crystal	$5.95		
Rhodonite	$5.95		
Sodalite	$5.95		
Unakite	$5.95		
Subtotal			
Tax (7% for RI customers)			
Shipping & Handling (*See shipping rates section*)			
TOTAL			

MISCELLANY			
Item	Price	Qty.	Total
Pouch	$3.95		
Matches: *10 small individual boxes*	$5.00		
Matches: *1 large box of 50 individual boxes*	$20.00		
Natural/Black Book Bag	$17.95		
Red/Black Book Bag	$17.95		
Hooded Sweatshirt, Blk	$30.00		
Hooded Sweatshirt, Red	$30.00		
L-Sleeve T, Black	$20.00		
L-Sleeve T, Red	$20.00		
S-Sleeve T, Black/W	$15.00		
S-Sleeve T, Black/R	$15.00		
S-Sleeve T, Dk H/R	$15.00		
S-Sleeve T, Dk H/W	$15.00		
S-Sleeve T, Red/B	$15.00		
S-Sleeve T, Ash/R	$15.00		
S-Sleeve T, Purple/W	$15.00		
Postcards – set of 12	$3.00		
Bookmarks – set of 12	$1.00		
Magnets – set of 3	$1.50		
Promo Pack	$7.00		
Subtotal			
Tax (7% sales tax for RI customers)			
Shipping & Handling (*See shipping rates section*)			
TOTAL			

SHIPPING & HANDLING CHARGES

BOOKS: One book, add $5.95. Each additional book add $1.50.

POUCH: One pouch, $3.95. Each additional pouch add $1.50.

MATCHES: Ten individual boxes, add $3.95.
One large box of fifty, add $6.00. Each additional large box add $7.95.

BOOKBAGS: $5.95 per bookbag.

BRACELETS: $3.95 per bracelet.

Send a check or money order payable in U. S. funds or credit card details to:

The Witches' Almanac, Ltd., PO Box 1292, Newport, RI 02840-9998

(401) 847-3388 (phone) • (888) 897-3388 (fax)
Email: info@TheWitchesAlmanac.com • www.TheWitchesAlmanac.com

ORDER FORM

Each timeless edition of *The Witches' Almanac* is unique.
Limited numbers of previous years' editions are available.

Item	Price	Qty.	Total
2017-2018 The Witches' Almanac – Water	$12.95		
2016-2017 The Witches' Almanac – Air	$12.95		
2015-2016 The Witches' Almanac – Fire	$12.95		
2014-2015 The Witches' Almanac – Earth	$12.95		
2013-2014 The Witches' Almanac – Moon	$11.95		
2012-2013 The Witches' Almanac – Sun	$11.95		
2011-2012 The Witches' Almanac – Stones, Powers of Earth	$11.95		
2010-2011 The Witches' Almanac – Animals Great & Small	$11.95		
2009-2010 The Witches' Almanac – Plants & Healing Herbs	$11.95		
2008-2009 The Witches' Almanac – Divination & Prophecy	$10.95		
2007-2008 The Witches' Almanac – Water	$9.95		
2003, 2004, 2005, 2006 issues of The Witches' Almanac	$8.95		
1999, 2000, 2001, 2002 issues of The Witches' Almanac	$7.95		
1995, 1996, 1997, 1998 issues of The Witches' Almanac	$6.95		
1993, 1994 issues of The Witches' Almanac	$5.95		
Dame Fortune's Wheel Tarot: A Pictorial Key	$19.95		
Magic: An Occult Primer	$24.95		
The Witches' Almanac Coloring Book	$12.00		
The Witchcraft of Dame Darrel of York, clothbound	$65.00		
The Witchcraft of Dame Darrel of York, delux numbered leatherbound	$145.00		
Aradia or The Gospel of the Witches	$16.95		
The Horned Shepherd	$16.95		
The ABC of Magic Charms	$12.95		
The Little Book of Magical Creatures	$12.95		
Greek Gods in Love	$15.95		
Witches All	$13.95		
Ancient Roman Holidays	$6.95		
Celtic Tree Magic	$7.95		
Love Charms	$6.95		
Love Feasts	$6.95		
Magic Charms from A to Z	$12.95		
Magical Creatures	$12.95		
Magic Spells and Incantations	$12.95		
Moon Lore	$7.95		
Random Recollections II, III or IV (circle your choices)	$3.95		
SALE: 13 Almanac back issues with free book bag and free shipping	$ 75.00		
20 Almanac back issues with free book bag and free shipping	$100.00		
The Rede of the Wiccae – Hardcover only	$49.95		
Keepers of the Flame	$20.95		
Subtotal			
Tax *(7% sales tax for RI customers)*			
Shipping & Handling *(See shipping rates section)*			
TOTAL			